Tatting
in LACE

Frontispiece Tatted
handkerchief, *circa* 1820.

Tatting in LACE

Mary Konior

Dryad Press Ltd
LONDON

ACKNOWLEDGMENT

With very special thanks: to Catherine Pickering and Teresa Withycombe, my daughters, for test-working the pattern directions; to Eleanor Adams, for allowing me to photograph her shuttles; to J & P Coats Ltd, for kindly supplying crochet cottons; to the English Lace School, for allowing me to photograph the parasol cover; to Betty Suter Feldman, of the Ring of Tatters, for information relating to the portrait of Mrs Seymour Fort; to Kathleen Gidden, of the Ring of Tatters, for allowing me to photograph tatting from her collection; to Patricia Knowlden, for, once upon a time, teaching me to tat; to Carl Konior, for assistance in tracing historic data; and to Trixie Sparrow, of the Ring of Tatters, for suggesting a source of design.

Illustration 2 is reproduced by courtesy of the Board of Trustees of the Victoria and Albert Museum. Illustration 61 is reproduced by kind permission of the Administrative Trustees of the Chevening Estate. All other illustrations and artwork are by the author.

© Mary Konior 1988
First published 1988

British Library Cataloguing in Publication Data
Konior, Mary
  Tatting in lace.
  1. Tatting. Manuals
  I. Title
  746.43'6
  ISBN 0-85219-722-5

Typeset by Servis Filmsetting Ltd
and printed in Great Britain by
The Bath Press Ltd
Bath
for the publishers
Dryad Press Ltd
8 Cavendish Square
London W1M 0AJ

Contents

6

Introduction

... two old gentlemen bore down on the booth, declaring in loud voices that they wanted ten miles of tatting. Well, after all, old gentlemen are better than no gentlemen at all, thought Scarlett, measuring out the tatting, and submitting demurely to being chucked under the chin.

She had . . . tatted yards of lace.

Margaret Mitchell, *Gone With the Wind* (1936)

When Scarlett tatted her yards of lace, she would not have been aware of the origin of the term. There is often, still, wild speculation about the source, but 'tat' was an old English expression common in Northern dialects for a knot, usually referring to a tangled knot in wool or hair. 'Tatting' is thus a synonym for knotting. The novelist Catherine Cookson, a native of Tyneside, uses 'tat' to describe a knot of hair, and it is significant that in the Lancashire cotton mills the man who removed knots from the finished cloth was known as a 'tatler'.

Tatting, which could also be described as shuttle lace, is a work of engaging charm. The shuttle provides a means for knotting thread in such a manner that the resultant lace forms in the hands.

Only one knot is used – a reversed double half-hitch, variously known as the Lark's Head or Cow Hitch, (and mercifully called a double stitch in written patterns). A knot of similar appearance is used in macramé, but the similarity is deceptive, as tatting is not all that it appears to be. The active thread which is cast around does not itself form the knot, but is an agent which converts a passive secondary thread into knot form. This conversion, referred to as 'the Transfer' by tatting enthusiasts, occasions great rejoicing when first mastered.

7

Historically, tatting is a development of an earlier practice used in embroidery, where a heavy thread or cord, knotted at close intervals like a string of beads, would be couched to fabric in order to add texture or outline to a design. Knots of different types were used in this way during the seventeenth and eighteenth centuries in Western Europe, and although few of the ensuing embroideries have survived, the pastime of *knotting*, as it was then called, was well documented in contemporary letters, diaries and verse.

The literary Dr Johnson is quoted by his biographer Boswell in 1784 as saying:

> Next to mere idleness I think knotting is to be reckoned in the scale of insignificance; though I once attempted to learn knotting. Dempster's sister endeavoured to teach me it; but I made no progress.

Presumably he couldn't manage 'the Transfer'.

Fashionable ladies carried conspicuous knotting shuttles on public occasions and would indulge in the pursuit at every opportunity. A list of ladies (given at the end of this book) who posed shuttle-in-hand for their portraits during the period 1740 to 1780, includes several princesses, countesses and a queen, among other distinguished ranks. In all the art of knotting seems to have lodged in some very good homes. Perhaps Dr Johnson was just jealous.

The progression from simple knotting to the more sophisticated tatting is difficult to date, for there was an obvious period of overlap when both were in favour.

According to Tina Frauberger, writing in 1919 in *Handbuch der Schiffchenspitze* (Handbook of Shuttle Lace), published directions appeared in the early eighteenth century in *Nutzbares, galantes und curioses Frauenzimmer-Lexicon* (which defies a polished translation but means a dictionary of useful and fancy women's work), 3rd edition 1739. Tina Frauberger interprets the directions as referring to shuttle lace rather than knotting, and if she is correct, then this must be the earliest evidence of genuine tatting.

By the beginning of the nineteenth century, tatted laces were being produced from a preliminary series of rings made yard upon yard like an endless daisy chain, and patiently sewn into circles. The profusion of picots which typifies these laces serves to camouflage signs of sewing, although the latter are always apparent at the back of the work. Needlepoint lace fillings were a common addition, and sometimes needlepoint bars or chains were also featured.

1 Early nineteenth-century tatting, from a collection owned by Kathleen Gidden

8

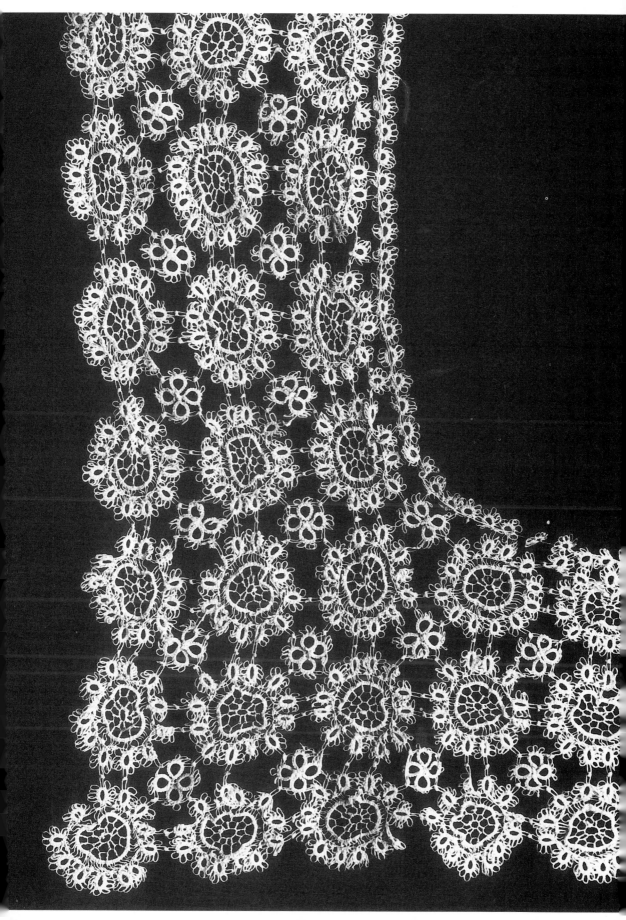

2 Irish tatting, 1883,
Victoria and Albert
Museum

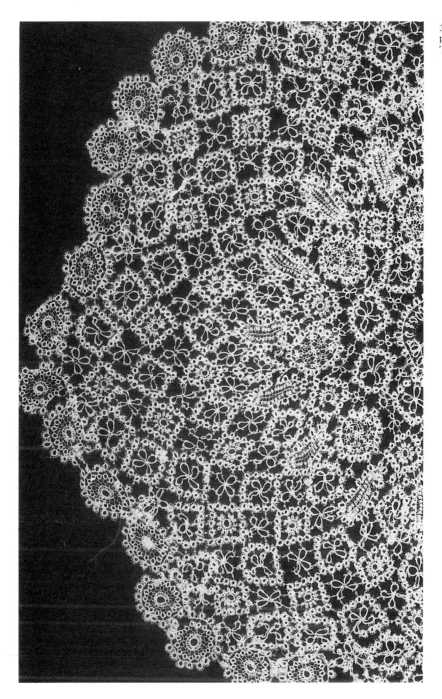

3 Nineteenth-century
parasol cover in tatting,
The English Lace School

4 Tatting made in China and purchased recently in Cape Town

Tatting may be formed entirely from rings, entirely from chains, or from a combination of both. The presence of true tatted chains (as opposed to needlepoint chains) can be a useful means of assessing the age of an antique specimen, as these were a development dating from 1864, and usually attributed to Eléonore Riego de la Branchardière – an Englishwoman. Riego was a famed 'Artiste in Needlework' who published a remarkable range of small books, including eleven on tatting, all now collector's items. The present method of joining rings with a shuttle was first mentioned in a publication of 1851, and this too offers a useful means for dating work.

To judge from *Gone With the Wind*, tatting was an accepted means of raising Confederate funds during the American Civil War. A more realistic commercial success followed when tatting was launched around Ardee in County Louth, as part of the general lacemaking industry which prospered in Ireland in the mid-nineteenth century.

Nowadays tatting can be purchased in many tourist areas. The shops of Venice are always well stocked. Modern commercial work can usually be traced to Chinese origins and can be identified by a typical use of crochet in the designs.

'What is the use of it?' is a challenge sometimes heard, yet no one ever asks this question of machine-made or bobbin lace, and tatting can be considered equal to any other form of lace for dress or household use. It is particularly suited to the English country house or 'Laura Ashley' look of cotton prints, ruffles and lace trimmings. Tatting, too, is exactly right for the dressy Edwardian-style blouse. A juxtaposition of pin-tucks, satin ribbon and lace on semi-transparent lawn or georgette is an old theme, but luscious.

Every striving hostess should own some tatting. It offers such an easy opening for conversation and flattery.

"The . . . napkins are wonderfully extravagant" cooed the journalist, proffering a small tape-recorder as if it were a packet of black Balkan Sobranie cigarettes. "Did you tat them yourself?"

Clive James, *Brilliant Creatures*, (Jonathan Cape, 1983)

CHAPTER ONE
Equipment for tatting

The basic requisites for tatting are a shuttle and a ball of thread. These need cost so little that many addicts stress the economy of their craft. Perhaps this aspect should be viewed with caution, for according to an old saying, 'The more a thrifty wife saves, the more her husband spends on other women'.

Antique shuttles are often exquisite and covetable. They were made of ivory, mother-of-pearl, tortoiseshell, and all sorts of precious and semi-precious materials. Iridescent shell or opal was always appreciated, as this would shimmer with reflected light during work. Knotting shuttles were larger than tatting shuttles and had open ends in order to accommodate the thicker threads of their day.

Tatting shuttles are quite small, usually $2\frac{1}{2}-2\frac{3}{4}$ inches (6–7 cm) in length, this being an optimum size for working at speed; too large a shuttle can be cumbersome and inhibit an even rhythm of work. The traditional tatting shuttle has points at each end which just meet, but are sufficiently flexible for easy winding. The classic test for utility is that a shuttle should hold its thread and not unwind when dangled, and this test should always be applied to an aged shuttle, as all too often the points weaken with maturity.

Modern shuttles are manufactured in various types of plastic, and models of a sophisticated design have a central spool which can be removed for winding. A small hook is a necessary item when tatting, and a tatting hook was formerly attached to a thumb ring which was worn on the left hand. The thumb ring is now obsolete and a steel crochet hook of approximately 1.5 mm (American size 7 or 8) makes a good substitute. Some shuttles have a hook incorporated into their design and set at one of the points, negating the need for a separate hook; a variation of the shuttle-cum-hook design is the tooth extension which replaces the hook, although many tatters consider this unsuitable for use with fine threads.

5 Antique knotting
shuttles of tortoiseshell
inlaid with gold and silver,
from a collection owned
by Eleanor Adams

Threads for tatting need to be smooth, hard, and evenly spun.
Mercerised crochet cottons are excellent. The thickest crochet
cotton that a traditional shuttle will accept is usually No. 10, and
the finest available, No. 150, is only just strong enough to
withstand the pull of a shuttle without snapping. Nos 10 and 20 are
recommended for beginners' use.

The size of thread for each pattern is given solely as a guide; there
is no reason why this should not be changed at the worker's
discretion, nor is it essential to keep to crochet cottons. Sewing
cottons, silk or polyester top-stitching threads, and many embroidery threads may all be used, although stitches will glide more neatly
into place with a mercerised or silk thread than with a matt thread.
It is becoming increasingly difficult to obtain crochet cottons other
than No. 20 in a range of colours. However, polyester top-stitching
thread is available in a wide colour spectrum, and is approximately
equal to No. 40 crochet cotton. Do not work too tightly when using

15

6 Antique tatting shuttles, of Chinese ivory and of horn, inlaid and made to simulate tortoiseshell, from a collection owned by Eleanor Adams

7 Tatting shuttles, old and new – ivory, bone, tortoiseshell, horn, mother-of-pearl, abalone shell, silver, brass, wood and plastic. The finely inlaid, slender shuttle is Tunbridge Ware; the shuttle with the tooth extension is Japanese plastic

polyester, as there is a slight but disadvantageous 'give' to the thread.

To fill a shuttle, tie the thread to its centre and wind as much as the shuttle will conveniently hold without the thread protruding beyond its sides. Hands should be immaculately clean, as it is important to keep threads in pristine condition during work. A removable central spool can be fitted to a sewing machine for fast winding.

Scissors, pins and needles and other general workbox items will also be useful when tatting.

CHAPTER TWO
How to tat

There was once a fallacy, and it lingers still, that the mystique of tatting could not be learned from the printed word, and that for some reason it had to be acquired in a face-to-face encounter. This no doubt stemmed from the fact that publications at the beginning of the present century were woefully inadequate at explanation.

Nowadays, we are more aware of the rationales of lucid instruction, and so the following directions include a carefully composed text and adequate diagrams – pop-up pictures could add no more. Nevertheless, a raw beginner must expect to devote considerable time to mastery of the basics, for the left hand is used a great deal in a manner which could present initial problems to a right-hander.

First practise 'the Transfer':

Take two lengths of string or coarse thread, smooth of surface and of different colours. Knot the two together and use thread B to form

1 Transfer of the half-hitch

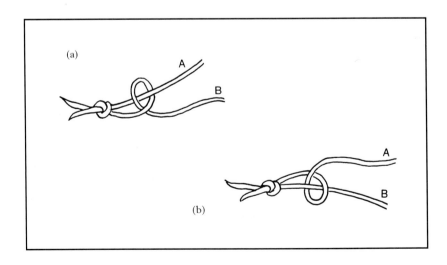

(a)

(b)

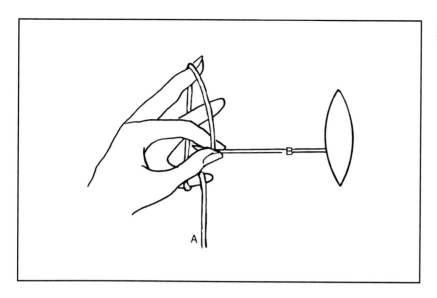

a half-hitch or loop on thread A (Fig. 1(a)). Grip the knot with the left hand and tug thread B sharply. The loop on thread B should transfer to thread A, and the original half-hitch has now become a half-stitch in tatting (Fig. 1(b)). In practice, thread B is wound on the shuttle and thread A is the thread from the ball or whatever source. Half-stitches are worked in pairs to form the double stitch which is the basis of all tatting.

METHOD 1

To make a chain of double stitches

Using two threads of different colours, wind the shuttle with B and leave A running from the ball. Knot both together, grip the knot in the left hand with the thumb and first finger, and take the ball thread A over the back of the outstretched fingers and around the fourth finger (Fig. 2). Place shuttle thread B in a loop over the top of the left hand and pass the shuttle upwards, under A and through the loop made by B (Fig. 3(a)). This will result in thread B looped on thread A as shown in Fig. 1(a). Transfer the loop to thread A, as shown in Fig. 1(b), with a sharp tug of the shuttle. It is essential that thread A is sufficiently slack to allow this, and the outstretched second finger should be dropped in order to slacken it. The transferred loop is now the first half-stitch. Slide it up next to the knot by gradually stretching the second finger outwards again (Fig. 3(b)). Hold the first half-stitch in position with the thumb.

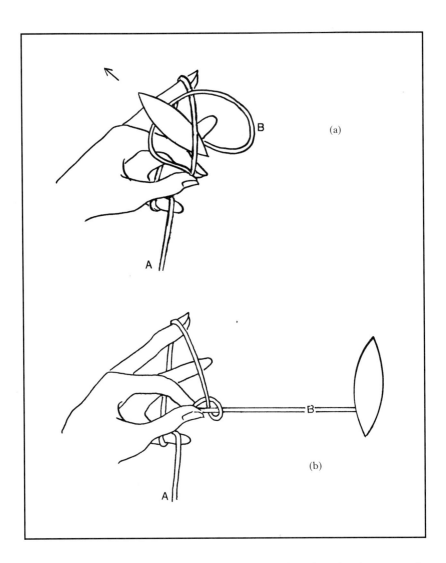

3 Making the first half-stitch

To make the second half-stitch, pass the shuttle downwards under A and over B (Fig. 4(a)). This will result in thread B looped on thread A (Fig. 4(b)). Note that the loop faces the opposite way to that shown in Fig. 1(a). Transfer this loop on thread B to thread A as before (Fig. 4(c)). The transferred loop is now the second half-stitch. Slide it up next to the first half-stitch, and note that one is the reverse of the other. Both together form the double stitch (Fig. 5).

Practise a series of double stitches, thus forming a chain. All stitches should slide easily on shuttle thread B.

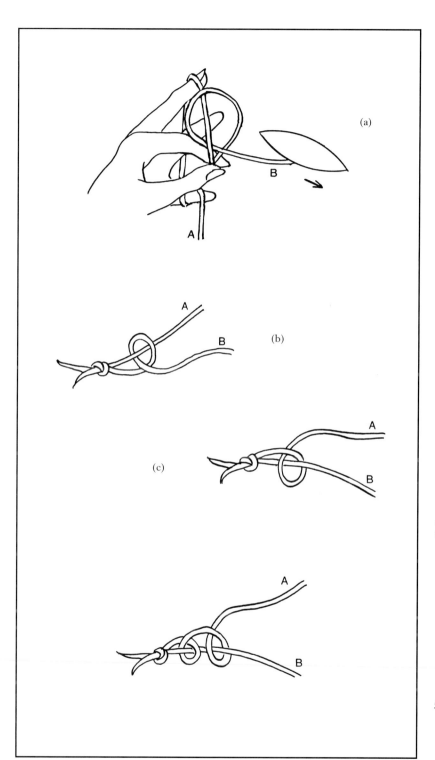

(a)

B

A

(b)

A

B

(c)

A

B

4 Making the second half-stitch

A

B

5 A double stitch

To make a picot

Leave a small space between stitches, the length of the space depending on the thickness of the thread used. When the stitches are pushed up together, the space forms a picot (Fig. 6).

To make a ring

The shuttle thread is used alone to make a ring. Abandon the ball thread, allowing it to hang loose, and wrap the shuttle thread completely around the outstretched fingers of the left hand to form a ring, gripping it together with the thumb and first finger (Fig. 7). Work a series of double stitches as shown for making a chain, although A and B are now different parts of the same thread. The ring thread A will gradually become smaller as work progresses, and the outstretched fingers of the left hand will be forced to contract. To enlarge the ring, stretch the fingers out again, still gripping with the thumb and first finger, so that extra thread is fed through to the ring. It is essential that all the double stitches should slide easily on thread B and, if they do not, it means that they have been incorrectly worked at some point, and that the transfer stages shown in Fig. 1(b) and Fig. 4(c) have been omitted. Mistakes can be unpicked with a hook or with a pin, but tatting will not unravel.

To complete and close the ring, slip it off the outstretched fingers, still gripping with the first finger and thumb, and gently pull the shuttle. The ring will close completely, provided that all double stitches are correctly worked (Fig. 8).

To construct a design

Tatted laces may consist of all rings, or of all chains, but most designs are a combination of both. If, after working a ring, pattern directions then require a chain, pick up the ball thread on the left hand and use both ball and shuttle threads. If, after working a chain, pattern directions then require a ring, drop the ball thread and take the shuttle thread on the left hand. When changing from rings to chains, and vice versa, begin each as closely to its predecessor as possible without leaving any thread or space between them. If a space is required, pattern directions will specify the exact amount. Similarly, when working a series of rings, do not leave a space between each unless this is specified. Usually, work is reversed each time that it changes from ring to chain, and vice versa, and this means turning the ring or chain just completed upside down before starting the next. Directions to reverse work will be given in the pattern.

22

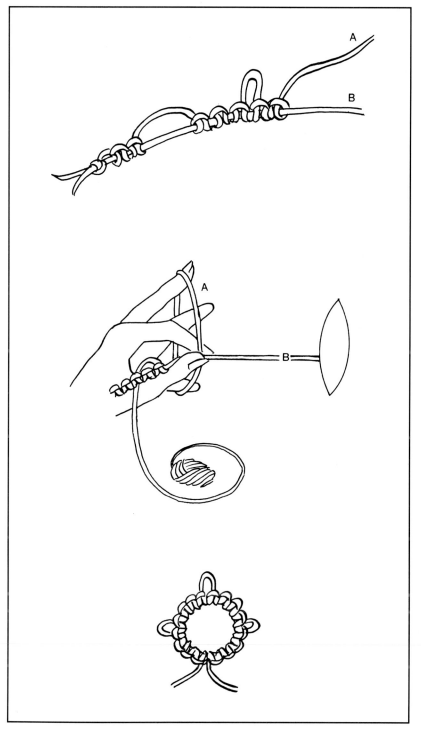

6 Making a picot

7 Holding the thread to start a ring

8 A closed ring

23

To join component parts

Rings and chains are joined to each other by the use of picots, and the method of joining is the same whether working a ring or chain. Insert the hook into a previously worked picot and catch thread A, pulling it out into a loop. Pass the shuttle through this loop (Fig. 9(a)). Tighten and position the loop so that it slides on thread B. The join is counted as a first half-stitch and is followed by a second half-stitch to complete it (Fig. 9(b)). This method of joining, using thread A, is the usual method of joining tatting.

In order to practise joining and to become familiar with the normal sequence of work in tatting, make a length of the traditional beginner's pattern (Fig. 9(c)). Using the shuttle thread only, make a ring of four double stitches, picot, four double stitches, picot, four double stitches, picot, four double stitches. * Reverse work and take up the ball thread on the left hand. Using both threads, make a chain of four double stitches, picot, four double stitches. Reverse work. Using the shuttle thread only, make a ring of four double stitches, join to the last picot of the previous ring (as shown in Figs 9(a) and 9(b)) and continue the ring with three double stitches, picot, four double stitches, picot, four double stitches. Repeat from * for the length required. There is no cast-off in tatting – just cut the two threads and tie them together.

Sometimes, a design will require the shuttle thread to be tied as a join, but this is unusual and will be specified in the pattern. For a shuttle thread join, insert the hook into a ready-made picot, catch the shuttle thread B and pull it out into a loop. Pass the shuttle through and tighten the resultant knot. It is a fixed knot which does not slide, and it does not count as a stitch (Fig. 10).

To ensure a good tension

Tatting should be firmly worked and should not be a lank cobweb. Close each ring well, and tighten each chain after it is worked by pushing the stitches well up together, but do not tighten tatting so much that shapes become distorted. Picots required for joins can be made smaller than ornamental picots as they need only be large enough for insertion of the hook. Eliminate unwanted spaces between rings and chains by being very careful with the position of the first half-stitch at the beginning of each ring or chain.

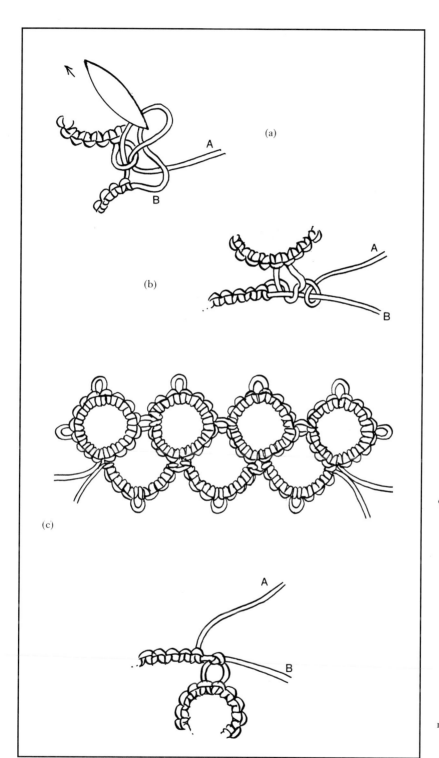

(a)

(b)

(c)

9 Joining tatting

10 A shuttle thread join

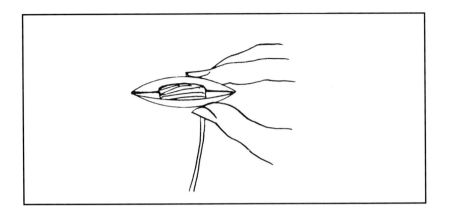

1 Holding the shuttle

METHOD 2

This is a quicker method of working which can with practice become very speedy, for the shuttle has a short and direct path to travel at each movement, rather than the more roundabout excursions of Method 1. However, it is difficult for a beginner to master, and for this reason it is better to learn using Method 1 and to advance to Method 2 later.

The differences are in Fig. 3(a) and Fig. 4(a) only, i.e. in the manner of passing the shuttle to make the preliminary half-hitch; all other processes are the same. The way in which the shuttle is held is important. Hold it with the thread leading from the back, using the thumb and first finger of the right hand (Fig. 11). Take shuttle thread B between the third and fourth fingers of the right hand, so that it catches on the tip of the fourth finger, keeping it taut. Pass the shuttle under B and under A, pushing it upwards against A which is also taut (Fig. 12(a)). Keeping the same grip on the shuttle, take it backwards under thread B. The tension of the pushing action should slip thread A over the top of the shuttle and back underneath in one movement, all without the finger and thumb being removed from the shuttle (Fig. 12(b)). At the same time, allow B to drop from the fourth finger and then from the rest of the hand. Thread B is now looped on thread A as in Fig. 1(a), ready to be transferred in the usual way to form a first half-stitch.

For the second half-stitch, pass the shuttle to the left, pressing it on top of thread A, which should be taut (Fig. 13). Pressure from the shuttle should cause thread A, underneath, to slip back over the top of the shuttle in one movement, without either finger or thumb being removed from the shuttle. Thread B is now looped on thread A as shown in Fig. 4(b), ready to be transferred in the usual way to form a second half-stitch.

26

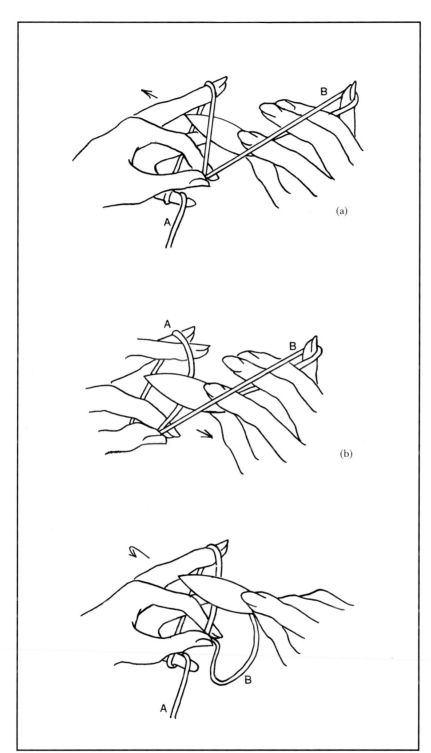

(a)

(b)

12 Making the first half-stitch

13 Making the second half-stitch

CHAPTER THREE
Special techniques

Many experienced tatters evolve their own particular wiles in pursuit of excellence, and indeed it is sometimes possible to recognise the maker from the style. Perhaps some of the following will help towards perfecting artistry.

CONNECTING A ROSETTE

A series of rings joined as a rosette can often present a problem with the final connecting picot, which so often becomes twisted. Hold the work as shown, with the last ring upright and incomplete in the hand, and the first ring to the right (Fig. 14(a)).

Fold the first ring forwards to the left, so that the back of it is facing (Fig. 14(b)). Give the joining picot of the first ring a half-twist backwards and upwards (Fig. 14(c)). Insert the hook from the front, complete the join as usual and finish the ring. This should result in a perfect join without unwanted twist.

STARTING WITHOUT A KNOT

When first learning, it is convenient to tie the ball thread and shuttle thread together in a knot, as it gives the fingers something to hold, but most proficient tatters will avoid knots as much as possible. When first filling the shuttle there is no need to sever the thread from shuttle to ball, only to tie the ends together again. However if making a fresh start and the ball and shuttle threads are already cut, a length can be unwound from the shuttle and wound back on the ball. Start as usual, and when the break in the ball thread is later reached, join as follows.

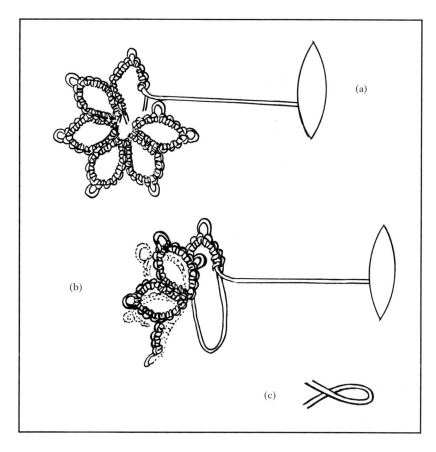

(a)

(b)

(c)

14 Joining a rosette

JOINING A THREAD – METHOD 1

This is a way of joining a new ball thread or a new shuttle thread, and it is best worked at the commencement of a ring or chain. For a chain, overlap the old and new ball threads sufficiently to wrap the whole overlap on the left hand, around the fourth finger, clutching tightly. Work three or four double stitches, then drop the old thread and continue with the new. For a ring, overlap the old and new shuttle threads so that both can encircle the hand, again clutching tightly, and proceed as given for the chain. The ends can be clipped once a ring is closed (Fig. 15), or once a chain is completed. The method gives a slight thickening where the thread is double, so to compensate for this fewer stitches need be worked than given in the pattern. Picots should not be worked with a double thread.

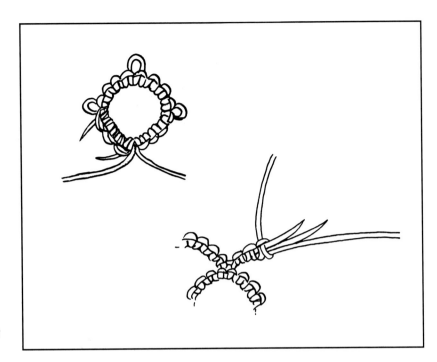

JOINING A THREAD – METHOD 2

Tie a knot and hide the two ends by running them alongside the
shuttle thread so that they are concealed by a few double stitches
(Fig. 16). This should be done at the beginning of a ring or chain,
and it is best achieved by using a hook to pull both ends through
each half-stitch before the latter is positioned and tightened. The
method can result in an extremely neat join, especially if the ends
are clipped at different lengths. An alternative is to take each end in
an opposite direction, running one into a chain and the other into a
ring, although of course this involves twice as much work.

OPENING A CLOSED RING

Most tatters admit defeat at this manoeuvre, as once a ring is closed
any attempt to open it again by pulling at its base will only tighten
the last stitch, so making the task impossible. However a closed ring
can be opened by easing the stitches apart elsewhere on its
circumference, at a picot, and gently pulling the running thread
revealed there (Fig. 17) with a hook or with tweezers. Concentrate
on easing the stitches to the right of the exposed running thread, as
a pull towards the left will tend to tighten the important last stitch.

30

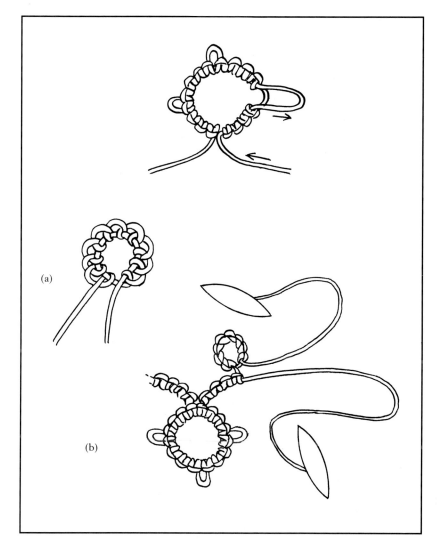

17 Opening a closed ring

(a)

(b)

18 A Josephine Knot

Once sufficient thread has been loosened, the stitches to the left can be shunted along until the loosened thread reaches the base of the ring. The ring can be then fully opened and stitches unpicked as required.

MAKING A JOSEPHINE KNOT

This is a survival from eighteenth-century knotting. To work a Josephine Knot (Fig. 18(a)) make a tiny ring using half-stitches instead of the usual double stitches. Most tatters choose the second

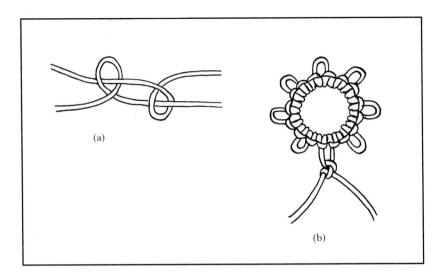

(a)

(b)

19 Making a lock stitch

half-stitch rather than the first, as this is quicker. Either may be selected, but it is essential to keep to the same choice throughout. Josephine Knots are often used to decorate chains, and in this case the ball thread must be wound on a second shuttle which is brought into use to work each Josephine Knot (Fig. 18(b)).

USING TWO SHUTTLES

For easy recognition, use shuttles of different colours or types. When working a chain, the main shuttle is held in the right hand, and the thread from the second shuttle wound on the left hand, in exactly the same way as the thread from a ball. If a Josephine Knot is required, drop the main shuttle, and take up the second shuttle on its own to work the Josephine Knot. Work is not reversed. On completion, change the second shuttle to ball-thread position and take up the main shuttle in the right hand again, ready to continue the chain. Note that the Josephine Knot stands on the outer rim of the chain, as shown in Fig. 18(b), and similarly it is possible to work a normal ring in the same position, also using the second shuttle.

LOCKING A STITCH

This is a procedure used to prevent a stitch from running on the shuttle thread. To work a lock stitch make a half-hitch preparatory to making a first half-stitch, but omit the transfer of the loop, thus making an incorrect half-stitch. Follow it with a correctly worked second half-stitch, and the two together have tied or locked the threads (Fig. 19(a)). A lock stitch can be useful for forming a false picot in order to complete a ring, and at the same time bring the two threads into position ready to start a chain on a following round (Fig. 19(b)).

FINISHING FINAL ENDS

Ends left on completion can be run in by overcasting or stab-stitching, inserting a needle through the heads of the nearest double stitches.

When using a very thick thread, the ends can be split into strands and each strand sewn in separately. As tatting is continually reversed during its production, the front of the rings and the back of the chains will be on the same side; thus a finished piece is reversible, without a definite right or wrong side, and both sides of the work should be equally neat.

WASHING AND PRESSING

As a final touch, tatting will benefit from being damped, for this will shrink natural fibres and generally improve tension, so making any imperfections less noticeable. While it is still damp, smooth the tatting out by hand on an absorbent cloth and straighten any wayward picots. An ornate lace can be pinned to shape with an array of pins around its edges. After being well shaped and flattened by hand, tatting can be left to dry naturally, and this is often the only treatment needed. If ironing is considered necessary, press under a cloth.

Soiled tatting usually responds to a good soak in a solution of washing powder, and heavily soiled white work can be boiled in the old-fashioned way in a saucepan – just a few minutes' fierce boil yields excellent results. Substantial articles of tatting can be safely machine washed if placed inside a pillow case or similar receptacle for protection. On no account should washed tatting be allowed to dry in a dishevelled state. Any twisted picots can easily be manipulated into shape whilst wet, whereas once dry the task becomes very tedious.

CHAPTER FOUR
Further types of tatting

To misquote a forgotten source, there is no subject, however simple, which, if studied with diligence and care, cannot be made complex. This maxim applies to tatting, although an increase in technical ingenuity will not necessarily be reflected as a relative increase in visual charm. Perhaps some natural law of spite is involved – one can be too clever. Nevertheless, the following are all fascinating.

TWISTED TATTING

This is also known as Spiral Tatting, and is worked with a series of half-stitches instead of the usual double stitches. Either the first half-stitch or the second half-stitch can be used, but it is essential to keep to the same type throughout. As work progresses, the heads of the half-stitches will twist around the shuttle thread to form a spiral. The method is very suitable for long chains (Fig. 20). A Josephine Knot is actually an example of a ring in Twisted Tatting, but as it is so small the twist is unobtrusive.

VICTORIAN SETS

A further development of Twisted Tatting, this is also known as Zig-Zag or Ric-Rac Tatting, as the twist continually changes direction. It is also called node stitch, from the little bumps or nodes which protrude.

Work, for example, four first half-stitches, four second half-stitches, four firsts, four seconds, and this will constitute two sets of four half-stitches (Fig. 21). All need to be meticulously counted, otherwise the sequence of the twists will be ruined. Many normal tatting patterns can be converted to this type, but it should be

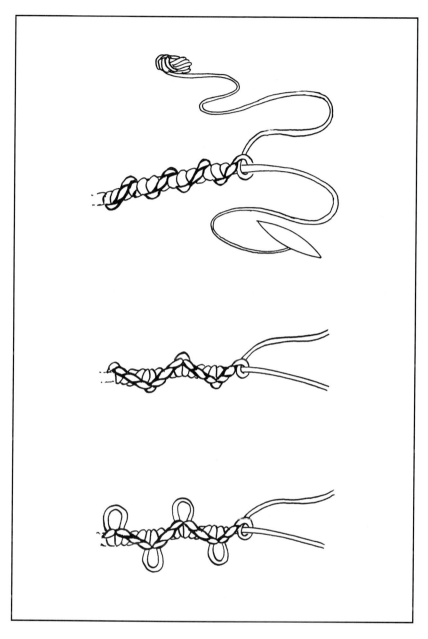

20 Twisted Tatting

21 Victorian Sets

22 Picots on Victorian Sets

remembered that the process of reversing work will also reverse the appearance of the sets, as these have a definite front and back. Picots can be placed at the change of direction of the twists (Fig. 22).

Some Victorian patterns called the first half-stitch 'plain' or 'French' stitch, and the second 'purl' or 'English stitch'.

PEARL TATTING

This seems to have been invented by Riego, 'pearl' being the Victorian word for 'picot'. To work Pearl Tatting, tie together two ball threads and the shuttle thread. Make a chain using each ball thread alternately, working a group of two or three double stitches with each thread, and reversing work at each change. It is possible to hold both ball threads simultaneously on the left hand, taking each in turn from the second finger, but it is important to reverse work in alternate directions, turning first towards oneself then back and away from oneself, in order that threads stay untangled. Large 'pearls' are formed across each group (Fig. 23). If the pearls are made extra long, the chain will resemble a braid of hairpin crochet, and can be substituted in hairpin-crochet designs.

Pearl Tatting lends itself to multi-coloured work, as does the even more intricate use of four ball threads (Fig. 24).

A variation of Pearl Tatting which appears never to have been given a name of its own, and for which 'pearl' seems a misnomer, is where the groups shown in Fig. 23 are enlarged and the threads between them shortened, so that the total form of the work changes completely (Fig. 25). If the ball threads are also wound on shuttles, then the groups can be embellished with rings or Josephine Knots (Fig. 26).

ROLL TATTING

Described as novel in 1916, this has a cord-like appearance. It usually looks better when used in conjunction with normal tatting than when used on its own.

To make a ring in Roll Tatting, start in the usual way and work a double stitch, then work a roll by passing the shuttle upwards through the ring (Fig. 27(a)). Tighten the shuttle thread so that the roll transfers to the ring thread, and continue to work rolls (Fig. 27(b)).

Two rolls are equivalent to one double stitch. Keep them well under control with the thumb, as they have a perverse tendency to become unrolled. Finish the ring with a double stitch before closing it. Similarly, begin and end each chain with a double stitch.

To make a picot, work a double stitch, then work a second double stitch with the picot between the two, before recommencing the roll. Similarly, work a double stitch before a join, and work the usual second half-stitch following the join.

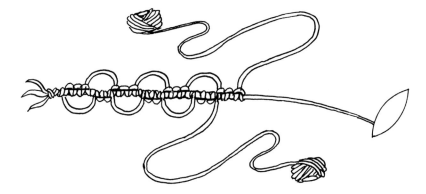

23 Pearl Tatting

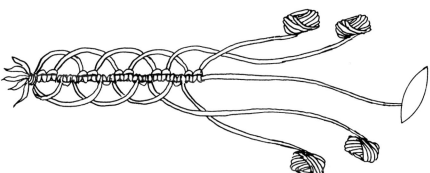

24 Pearl Tatting using
four ball threads

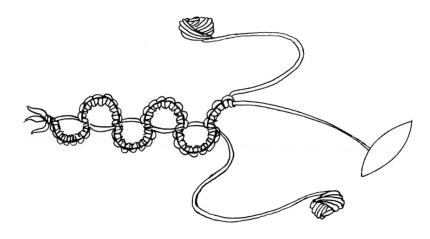

25 A variation of Pearl
Tatting

26 Pearl Tatting using
extra shuttles

27 Roll Tatting

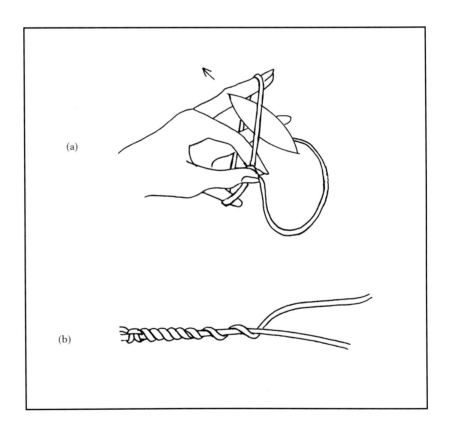

(a)

(b)

CHAPTER FIVE
The patterns

READING THE PATTERNS

The abbreviations used are as follows;
ds double stitch
hs half stitch
p picot
rw reverse work
Letters of the alphabet are used to identify particular rings and
chains whenever this is necessary to clarify meaning.

Instructions to tie ball and shuttle threads before commencement
are omitted as the presence of a chain infers the use of both and,
whilst it is convenient for a learner to tie the two threads together in
a knot, there are better ways of commencing as tatting skills
progress.

Picots are counted in the order in which they were originally
worked unless other directions are given.

The photographs have been chosen for clarity of illustration, and
should be sufficiently explanatory in the event of any ambiguity in
the written directions.

Patterns marked with a dagger (†) are suggested for beginners,
although raw beginners may prefer to use thicker threads than
shown in the original.

8 Nursing sister's cap
trimmed with *Eléonore*

9 Antique brooch frame
inset with *Bryony*

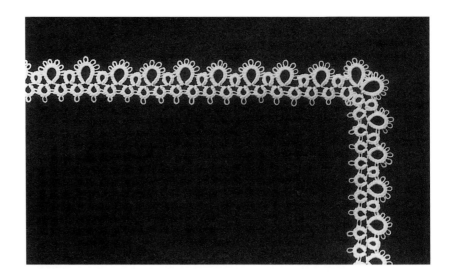

10 *Eléonore*

Eléonore†

Using crochet cotton No. 40, the edging measures $\frac{3}{4}$ inch (2 cm) in width.

This pattern is from Riego's *Tatting. Edgings and Insertions*, 1866, and is still a favourite. Examples can sometimes be found on antique dolls' clothes and on underwear of the period. Riego called it *Etruscan Border*, which suggests that it may have originated in Italy. The directions are exactly as given in the Victorian text. 'Oeillet' is the French term for 'eyelet', 'commence a loop' means 'start a ring' and 'pearl' means 'picot'.

1st Oeillet – Commence a loop, work 4 double, 1 pearl, 4 double, 1 pearl, 4 double, draw it close. Turn the oeillet on the other side, and keep it under the thumb, so that the foundation thread is at the top; and for the

2nd Oeillet – Commence a loop, work 3 double, 1 pearl, 3 double, 1 pearl, 3 double, 1 pearl, 3 double, draw it close. Turn this oeillet down, so as to bring the 1st oeillet at the top, and for the

* 1st Oval – Commence a loop, 5 double, join to the last pearl loop of the 1st oeillet, then 2 double, (1 pearl and 2 double, 6 times), 3 double more, draw it close. Turn this oval down, keep the 2nd oeillet above; and for the

3rd Oeillet – Commence a loop, work 3 double, join to the last pearl loop of the 2nd oeillet, then 3 double, 1 pearl, 3 double, 1 pearl, 3

42

double, draw close. Turn as before, keeping the oval above.

4th Oeillet – Commence a loop, 4 double, join to the last pearl loop of the oval, then 4 double, 1 pearl, 4 double, draw close, and reverse the work as before.

5th Oeillet – Commence a loop, 3 double, join to the last pearl loop of the 3rd Oeillet, then 3 double, 1 pearl, 3 double, 1 pearl, 3 double, draw close. Reverse the work, and repeat from * at the oval.

Corner
Work an oval with 8 pearls instead of the usual 6. Work a second similar oval immediately afterwards, joining to the last picot of the previous oval. Continue as before.

11 *Hedgerow*

Hedgerow

Using crochet cotton No. 20, the edging measures $1\frac{3}{4}$ inches (4.5 cm) in width and will adapt to a curve.

(First Flower) Ring A of 7 ds, p, (4 ds, p) twice, 7 ds.
* Ring B of 7 ds, join to last picot of previous ring, (4 ds, p) twice, 7 ds.
Repeat Ring B twice more, to complete flower, rw.
Chain A of 11 ds, p, 7 ds.

43

Ring C of 6 ds, p, 3 ds, p, 6 ds, rw.
Chain B of 5 ds, join to top picot of last ring of flower, 5 ds, p, 5 ds, rw.
Ring C of 6 ds, join to last picot of previous Ring C, 3 ds, p, 6 ds.
Chain C of 7 ds, p, 11 ds, rw.

(Second Flower) Ring A of 7 ds, p, 4 ds, join to Chain B, 4 ds, p, 7 ds.
Ring B of 7 ds, join to last picot of previous ring, 4 ds, join to 3rd ring of previous flower, 4 ds, p, 7 ds.
Complete flower as before. Do not reverse work.
Chain D of 7 ds, join to last picot of previous ring, (7 ds, p) twice, 7 ds.

(Third Flower) Ring A of 7 ds, join to last picot of Chain D, (4 ds, p) twice, 7 ds.
Complete flower as First Flower, rw.
Chain A of 11 ds, join to Chain C, 7 ds.
Ring C as previous Ring C, rw.
Chain B as before.
Ring C as previous Ring C. Do not reverse work.
Chain C as before.

Work a Fourth Flower as Second Flower, rw.
Chain E of 11 ds, p, 4 ds, p, 11 ds, rw.
(First Flower) Ring A of 7 ds, p, 4 ds, join to top picot of last ring of Fourth Flower, 4 ds, p, 7 ds.

Repeat from * for the length required, ending with a Fourth Flower for the corner. Do not reverse work.

Corner
Chain D of 7 ds, join to last picot of Fourth Flower, (7 ds, p) twice, 7 ds.
Continue from Third Flower as before.

Hoop-la

Using crochet cotton No. 20, the edging measures $\frac{5}{8}$ inch (1.5 cm) in width and will adapt to a curve.

This pattern is from Riego's *Exhibition Tatting Book*, 1862, and directions are exactly as given in the Victorian text. 'Rosette' and 'oval' are normal rings, 'commence a loop' means start a ring and 'pearl' means picot. All joins to the centre rosette are shuttle thread joins as shown in Fig. 10.

Centre Rosette – Fill the shuttle and commence a loop, work 2 double stitches, then (1 pearl and 2 double alternately 7 times), draw the loop quite close and turn the rosette down under the left finger and thumb,

1st Oval – Commence a loop, work 2 double, 1 pearl, 3 double, 1 pearl, 3 double, 1 pearl, 2 double; draw the loop close; join to the 1st pearl loop of the centre rosette.

* 2nd Oval – Commence, work 2 double, join to the last pearl loop of the 1st oval, 7 double, 1 pearl, 2 double; draw close; join to the next pearl loop of the centre rosette. Work two ovals more the same as the last, and for the

5th Oval – Commence, work 2 double, join to the last oval, 3 double, 1 pearl, 3 double, 1 pearl, 2 double; draw close; join to the next pearl loop of the rosette, then pass the cotton at the back of the

45

last oval and join to the centre pearl loop of it, keeping the cotton at the back so as not to show on the right side.

2nd Centre Rosette – Commence a loop, leaving a quarter of an inch of cotton from the last joining, work 2 double, (1 pearl and 2 double 7 times); draw close; turn the rosette down, and for the

1st Oval – Commence, work 2 double, 1 pearl, 3 double, join to the last oval at the pearl loop already attached, then 3 double, 1 pearl, 2 double, draw close; join to the 1st pearl loop of the centre rosette; the quarter of an inch of cotton left is to be kept at the back of this oval.

Repeat from * and continue for the length required.

Corner
Work 2 extra ovals on the usual rosette, then continue as before.

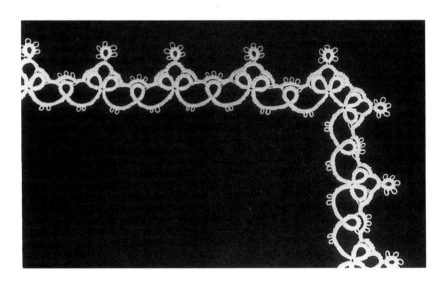

13 *Leapfrog*

Leapfrog

Using crochet cotton No. 40, the edging measures $1\frac{1}{8}$ inches (3 cm) in width and will adapt to a curve. Wind the ball thread on a second shuttle for the Second Row.

First Row
* Ring A of (6 ds, p) twice, 6 ds, rw.
Chain A of 7 ds, p, 2 ds, p, 9 ds, rw.
Ring B of (6 ds, p) twice, 6 ds.
Ring C as Ring A.
Chain B of 9 ds, p, 2 ds, p, 7 ds, rw.
Repeat from * for the length required, ending with Ring C for the corner.

Corner:
Chain of 6 ds, rw.
Rings B and C as before.
Continue from Chain B as before.

Second Row
Using main shuttle, join to first picot of first Ring A:
* Chain A of (2 ds, p) 3 times, 2 ds, join main shuttle thread to second picot of same ring, 2 ds, join main shuttle thread to first picot of next Ring B.
Chain B of 6 ds, join main shuttle thread to second picot of same ring, 4 ds.

Using second shuttle:
Ring of (2 ds, p) 5 times, 2 ds.
Using main shuttle:
Chain C of 4 ds, join main shuttle thread to first picot of next Ring C, 6 ds, join main shuttle thread to second picot of same ring, 2 ds, join main shuttle thread to first picot of next ring.
Repeat from * as required, omitting Chain A at the corner as shown.

Marigold

Using crochet cotton No. 60, the edging measures 1 inch (2.5 cm) in width.

Ring A of 5 ds, p, 6 ds, p, 11 ds, rw.
Chain A of 7 ds, p, 11 ds.
Ring B of 10 ds, p, (2 ds, p) twice, 6 ds.
* Ring C of 6 ds, join to last picot of previous ring, (2 ds, p) 4 times, 7 ds.

Ring D of 7 ds, join to last picot of previous ring, (2 ds, p) 4 times, 7 ds.

Ring E of 7 ds, join to last picot of previous ring, 2 ds, p, 6 ds, p, 6 ds.

Ring F of 6 ds, join to last picot of previous ring, 4 ds, p, 10 ds, rw.

Chain B of 9 ds, join to top picot of Ring A, 9 ds, p, 3 ds.

Ring A as before.

Chain A of 7 ds, join to Ring F, 11 ds.

Ring B of 10 ds, join to Ring E, (2 ds, p) twice, 6 ds.

Repeat from * for the length required, ending with Ring F for the corner.

Corner

Chain B of 9 ds, join to top picot of Ring A, 9 ds, p, 3 ds, small p, 1 ds, rw.

Chain A of 7 ds, join to Ring F, 11 ds.

Ring G of 10 ds, join to Ring E, (2 ds, p) twice, 7 ds.

Ring H of 7 ds, join to last picot of previous ring, (2 ds, p) 4 times, 9 ds.

Ring 1 of 9 ds, join to last picot of previous ring, (2 ds, p) 5 times, 9 ds.

Ring J of 9 ds, join to last picot of previous ring, (2 ds, p) 4 times, 7 ds.

Rings E and F as before.

Chain C of 15 ds, join to small picot of Chain B.

Ring A as before.

Chain A of 7 ds, join to Ring F, 11 ds.

Ring B of 10 ds, join to Ring E, (2 ds, p) twice, 6 ds.

Continue from * as before.

15 *Orchard*

Orchard†

Using crochet cotton No. 60, the edging measures $\frac{5}{8}$ inch (1.5 cm) in width and will adapt to a curve.

Ring A of 6 ds, p, 2 ds, p, 4 ds.
* Ring B of 4 ds, join to last picot of previous ring, 4 ds, p, 4 ds, rw.
Chain A of 6 ds, p, 6 ds, rw.
Ring C of 4 ds, join to Ring B, 4 ds, p, 4 ds.
Ring D of 4 ds, join to Ring C, 2 ds, p, 6 ds, rw.
Chain B of (6 ds, p) twice, 4 ds, rw.
Ring E of 6 ds, join to Ring D, 6 ds, p, (2 ds, p) 3 times, 6 ds.
Ring F of 6 ds, join to last picot of Ring E, (2 ds, p) twice, 6 ds.
Ring G of 6 ds, join to last picot of Ring F, (2 ds, p) 3 times, 6 ds, p, 6 ds, rw.
Chain C of 4 ds, join to last picot of Chain B, 6 ds, p, 6 ds, rw.
Ring H of 6 ds, join to last picot of Ring G, 2 ds, p, 4 ds.
Repeat from * for the length required, ending with Ring G for the corner.

Corner
Chain of 4 ds, join to last picot of Chain B, 4 ds, p, 4 ds, rw.
Ring E of 6 ds, join to last picot of Ring G, 6 ds, p, (2 ds, p) 3 times, 6 ds.
Rings F and G as before.
Chain C of 4 ds, join to previous chain, 6 ds, p, 6 ds, rw.
Continue from Ring H as before.

49

Piecrusts

Using crochet cotton No. 60, the edging measures $\frac{5}{8}$ inch (1.5 cm) in width.

First Row
* Ring A of (5 ds, p) twice, 5 ds, rw.
Chain of 5 ds, p, 2 ds, p, 5 ds, rw.
Ring B of 5 ds, p, (3 ds, p) twice, 5 ds, rw.
Chain as before.
Repeat from * for the length required, ending with Ring B for the corner. Do not reverse work.

Corner:
Work a second Ring B. Reverse work.
Chain of 5 ds, join to last picot of previous chain, 2 ds, p, 5 ds, rw.
Continue from Ring A as before.

Second Row
Join to first picot of first Ring A.
* Chain A of 3 ds, p, 3 ds, join shuttle thread to next picot of same ring, 2 ds, join shuttle thread to first picot of next ring.
Chain B of 3 ds, p, (2 ds, p) 4 times, 3 ds, join shuttle thread to last picot of same ring, 2 ds, join shuttle thread to first picot of next ring.

Repeat from * as required, working Chain B twice at the corner as shown.

50

Scarlett†

Using crochet cotton No. 60, the edging measures $\frac{5}{8}$ inch (1.5 cm) in width and will adapt to a curve. This Victorian favourite was equally well-known in America. There were several minor variants as the stitch counts can be altered easily. Former patterns did not include corners – the tatting was gathered instead.

Leave a space of $\frac{1}{8}$ inch (3 mm) between all rings.
Ring A of (3 ds, p) 3 times, 3 ds, rw.
* Ring B of 4 ds, p, 4 ds, rw.
Ring A of 3 ds, join to last picot of previous Ring A, (3 ds, p) twice, 3 ds, rw.
Ring C of 4 ds, join to previous Ring B, (2 ds, p) 6 times, 4 ds, rw.
Ring A as previous Ring A.
Ring D of 4 ds, join to last picot of Ring C, 4 ds, rw.
Ring A as previous Ring A.
Repeat from * for the length required ending with Ring D for the corner. Do not reverse work.

Corner
Ring B as before, but do not reverse work.
Join shuttle thread to last picot of previous Ring A.
Ring C as before.
Ring A of 3 ds, join to centre picot of previous Ring A, (3 ds, p) twice, 3 ds, rw.
Repeat from Ring D as before.

51

Speedwell

Using crochet cotton No. 60, the edging measures $\frac{3}{4}$ inch (2 cm) in width and will adapt to a curve. The 'cord' is a long twisted picot which should be approximately 3 times longer than the other picots – cut a slip of card as a gauge for measurement.

Ring A of (3 ds, p) twice, 6 ds, rw.
* Chain A of 8 ds, p, 8 ds, rw.
Ring B of 10 ds, join to last picot of previous ring, (2 ds, p) twice, 6 ds.
Ring C of 6 ds, join to last picot of previous ring, (2 ds, p) 6 times, 6 ds.
Ring D of 6 ds, join to last picot of previous ring, (2 ds, p) 3 times, 2 ds, long p, 2 ds, p, 6 ds.
Ring E of 6 ds, join to last picot of previous ring, (2 ds, p) twice, 10 ds, rw.
Chain B of 8 ds, p, 4 ds, join shuttle thread to last picot of Ring E, 4 ds, p, 8 ds, rw.
Ring F of 3 ds, join to long picot after twisting it 4 times, (3 ds, p) twice, 3 ds.
Ring G of 3 ds, join to last picot of previous ring, 3 ds, p, 6 ds, rw.
Repeat from * for the length required, ending with Ring C for the corner.

Corner
Repeat Ring C twice more.
Rings D and E as before.

Chain B of 8 ds, join to Chain A, 4 ds, join shuttle thread to last
picot of Ring E, 4 ds, p, 8 ds, rw.
Continue from Ring F as before.

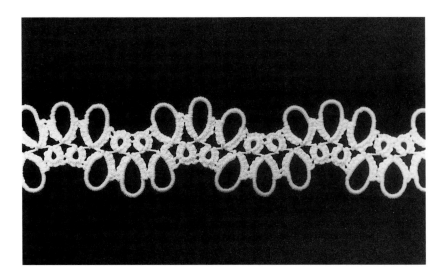

19 Acorns

Acorns

Using crochet cotton No. 10, the braid measures 1 inch (2.5 cm) in width and will adapt to a curve. This is an example of Roll Tatting as shown in Fig. 27.

Ring A of 3 ds, (p, 3 ds) twice, rw.
Ring B of 5 ds, p, 1 ds, 26 rolls, 1 ds, p, 5 ds, rw.
* Ring C of 3 ds, join to Ring A, 3 ds, p, 3 ds, rw.
Ring D of 5 ds, join to Ring B, 1 ds, 26 rolls, 1 ds, p, 5 ds, rw.
Ring E of 5 ds, join to Ring C, 1 ds, 26 rolls, 1 ds, p, 5 ds, rw.
Ring A of 3 ds, join to Ring D, 3 ds, p, 3 ds, rw.
Ring B of 5 ds, join to Ring E, 1 ds, 26 rolls, 1 ds, p, 5 ds, rw.

Repeat from * for the length required.

20 *Bumble-bee*

Bumble-bee†

Using crochet cotton No. 20, the braid measures $\frac{3}{4}$ inch (2 cm) in width.

Ring A of 7 ds, p, (2 ds, p) 4 times, 5 ds.
Ring B of 5 ds, join to last picot of previous ring, 2 ds, p, 5 ds.
Ring C of 5 ds, join to previous ring, (2 ds, p) 4 times, 7 ds, rw.
Ring D as Ring A.
Ring E as Ring B.
Ring F as Ring C.
* Ring A of 7 ds, join to last picot of Ring C, (2 ds, p) 4 times, 5 ds.
Rings B and C as before.
Ring D of 7 ds, join to last picot of Ring F, (2 ds, p) 4 times, 5 ds.
Rings E and F as before.

Repeat from * for the length required.

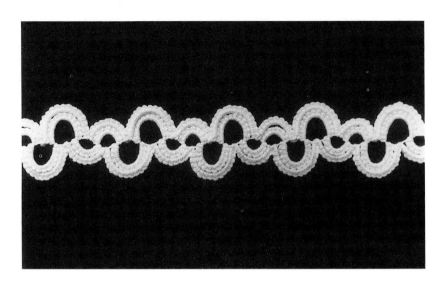

Chaingang

Using crochet cotton No. 10, the braid measures 1 inch (2.5 cm) in width and will adapt to a curve. The foundation is a variation of Pearl Tatting as shown in Fig. 25, and uses two ball threads.

Foundation Row
Tie the two ball threads and the shuttle thread together.
Using ball A: Chain of 8 ds, rw.
* Using ball B: Space of $\frac{1}{4}$ inch (6 mm), chain of 8 ds, rw.
Using ball A: Space as before, chain of 14 ds, rw.
Using ball B: Space as before, chain of 14 ds, rw.
Using ball A: Space as before, chain of 8 ds, rw.
Repeat from * for the length required. Do not finish off but continue with the outer row.

Outer Row (using one ball only)
* Chain of 10 ds (to lie over 8 ds), join shuttle thread to next space.
Chain of 16 ds (to lie over 14 ds), join shuttle thread to next space.
Repeat from * all along.

Work the opposite Outer Row to match.

Convolvulus

Using crochet cotton No. 20, the lace measures $1\frac{1}{4}$ inches (3.5 cm) in width.

Ring A of 3 ds, p, 6 ds, p, (3 ds, p) 4 times, 3 ds, rw.
Chain A of 3 ds, p, 12 ds, p, 3 ds, join shuttle thread to last picot (counting in the order worked) of Ring A.
Chain B of 3 ds, join to last picot of Chain A, 12 ds, p, 3 ds, join shuttle thread to next picot of Ring A.
Chain C of 3 ds, join to Chain B, 6 ds, p, (3 ds, p) twice, 3 ds, join shuttle thread to next picot of Ring A.
Chain D of 3 ds, join to last picot of Chain C, 3 ds, p, 12 ds, join shuttle thread to next picot of Ring A, rw.
Chain E of 3 ds, p, 15 ds, p, 3 ds, rw.
* Ring A of 3 ds, join to Chain D, 6 ds, join to nearest picot of Chain C, (3 ds, p) 4 times, 3 ds, rw.
Chain A of 3 ds, join to Chain E, 12 ds, p, 3 ds, join shuttle thread to last picot of Ring A.
Chains B, C and D as before.
Chain E of 3 ds, join to adjacent Chain C of previous flower, 15 ds, p, 3 ds, rw.

Repeat from * for the length required.

Corn and Chaff†

Using crochet cotton No. 20, the braid measures $\frac{5}{8}$ inch (1.5 cm) in width.

Ring A of 9 ds, p, 7 ds, p, 2 ds.
Ring B of 2 ds, join to last picot of Ring A, (1 ds, p) 5 times, 3 ds, rw.
Ring C as Ring A.
Ring D of 2 ds, join to last picot of Ring C, (1 ds, p) 5 times, 3 ds, rw.
* Ring A of 9 ds, join to last picot of previous Ring B, 7 ds, p, 2 ds.
Ring B of 2 ds, join to last picot of previous Ring A, (1 ds, p) 5 times, 3 ds, rw.
Ring C of 9 ds, join to last picot of previous Ring D, 7 ds, p, 2 ds.
Ring D of 2 ds, join to last picot of previous Ring C, (1 ds, p) 5 times, 3 ds, rw.

Repeat from * for the length required.

Honeysuckle†

Using crochet cotton No. 20, the lace measures $1\frac{1}{2}$ inches (4 cm) in width.

Ring A of 5 ds, p, 2 ds, p, 5 ds.
Ring B of 5 ds, join to last picot of previous ring, (2 ds, p) 3 times, 7 ds.
Ring C of 7 ds, join to last picot of previous ring, (2 ds, p) 5 times, 7 ds.
Ring D of 7 ds, join to last picot of previous ring, (2 ds, p) 3 times, 5 ds.
Ring E of 5 ds, join to last picot of previous ring, 2 ds, p, 5 ds, rw.
Ring F as Ring A.
Ring G as Ring B.
Ring H as Ring C.
Ring I as Ring D.
Ring J as Ring E,
* Ring A of 5 ds, join to Ring E, 2 ds, p, 5 ds.
Ring B of 5 ds, join to Ring A, 2 ds, join to corresponding picot of Ring D, (2 ds, p) twice, 7 ds.
Rings C, D and E as before.
Ring F of 5 ds, join to Ring J, 2 ds, p, 5 ds.
Ring G of 5 ds, join to Ring F, 2 ds, join to corresponding picot of Ring I, (2 ds, p) twice, 7 ds.
Rings H, I and J as before.

Repeat from * for the length required.

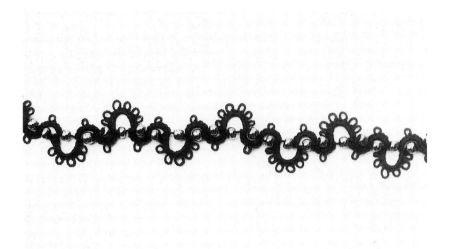

25 Nightshade

Nightshade

Using crochet cotton No. 20, the braid measures $\frac{3}{4}$ inch (2 cm) in width and will adapt to a curve. This is a variation of Pearl Tatting as shown in Fig. 25. Use two ball threads with an equal number of small beads threaded on each before starting.

Tie the two ball threads and the shuttle thread together.
* Using ball A: Chain of (2 ds, p) 6 times, 2 ds, rw.
Using ball B: Slip up a bead, chain of 4 ds, p, 4 ds, rw.
Using ball A: Slip up a bead, chain of 4 ds, p, 4 ds, rw.
Using ball B: Slip up a bead, chain of (2 ds, p) 6 times, 2 ds, rw.
Using ball A: Slip up a bead, chain of 4 ds, p, 4 ds, rw.
Using ball B: Slip up a bead, chain of 4 ds, p, 4 ds, rw.

Repeat from * adding a bead at every chain.

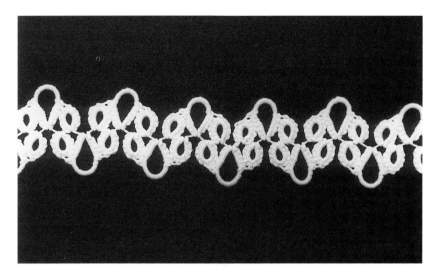

Nutmegs

Using crochet cotton No. 10, the braid measures 1 inch (2.5 cm) in width and will adapt to a curve. This is an example of Roll Tatting as shown in Fig. 27.

Ring A of 6 ds, p, 6 ds, rw.
Ring B as Ring A.
* Ring C of 5 ds, join to Ring A, 1 ds, 20 rolls, 1 ds, p, 5 ds, rw.
Ring A as before.
Ring B of 6 ds, join to Ring C, 6 ds, rw.

Repeat from * for the length required.

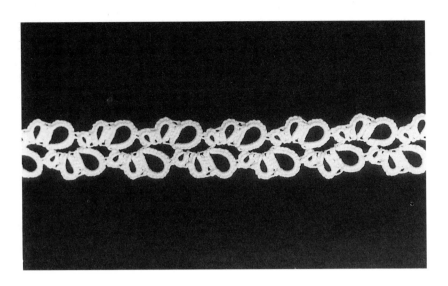

Three Wishes†

Using crochet cotton No. 20, the braid measures $\frac{3}{4}$ inch (2 cm) in width.

Ring A of (3 ds, p) twice, 3 ds.
Ring B of 3 ds, join to last picot of previous ring, 6 ds, p, 6 ds.
Ring C of 6 ds, join to previous ring, 9 ds, p, 9 ds, rw.
Ring D as Ring A.
Ring E as Ring B.
Ring F as Ring C.
* Ring A of 3 ds, join to previous Ring C, 3 ds, p, 3 ds.
Rings B and C as before.
Ring D of 3 ds, join to previous Ring F, 3 ds, p, 3 ds.
Rings E and F as before.

Repeat from * for the length required.

Trellis

Using crochet cotton No. 10, the strip measures 1½ inches (4 cm) in width. This is an example of Victorian Sets, as shown in Fig. 21.

First Row
* Ring A of 8 ds, p, 8 ds, rw.
Chain of (4 first hs, 4 second hs) 3 times (i.e., 3 sets of 4 hs), small picot, 3 sets of 4 hs, rw.
Ring B of 8 ds, join to Ring A, 8 ds.

Repeat from * for the length required.

Second Row
* Ring A of 8 ds, p, 8 ds, rw.
Chain of 3 sets of 4 hs, join to small picot of corresponding chain of First Row, 3 sets of 4 hs, rw.
Ring B of 8 ds, join to Ring A, 8 ds.

Repeat from * all along, joining to each chain in turn.

Alexandra

Using crochet cotton No. 40, the collar measures $2\frac{3}{4}$ inches (7 cm) in width; length and curvature are adjustable. The design consists of two half-collars, and matching cuffs can be made similarly.

First Motif
Centre ring of (2 ds, p) 13 times, 2 ds. Work lock stitch to form a 14th picot.
Chain A of 10 ds, rw.
* Ring A of 5 ds, p, 5 ds, rw.
Chain B of 6 ds, rw.
Ring B of 7 ds, p, 7 ds, rw.
Chain C of (3 ds, p) 5 times, 3 ds, join shuttle thread to picot of previous ring.
Chain D of 6 ds, join shuttle thread to picot of Ring A.
Chain E of 10 ds, join shuttle thread to next picot on centre ring.
Chain F of 10 ds, join in parallel to Chain E at junction with Ring A, rw.
Ring A, Chain C, Chain E and Chain F as before.
Repeat from * three times more, omitting the final Chain F to finish.

Second Motif
Work centre ring, Chain A, Ring A, Chain B and Ring B as before.
Chain C of (3 ds, p) twice, 3 ds, join to corresponding picot on last Chain C of First Motif, 3 ds, join to next picot of same chain, 3 ds, p, 3 ds, and complete motif as before.

Join a series of five motifs, or number required, for each half-collar.

Neck Edging

First Row
Ring A of 5 ds, p, 5 ds, p, 9 ds, rw.
Chain A of 9 ds, join to second picot (counting in the order worked) of first Chain C of First Motif, 3 ds, join to first picot of same chain, 9 ds, join shuttle thread to last picot of Ring A, rw.
* Ring A as before.
Chain B of 12 ds, join shuttle thread to last picot of previous Ring A, rw.
Ring A as before.
Chain C of 6 ds, rw.
Ring B of 7 ds, p, 7 ds, rw.

Chain D of 8 ds, join to second free picot of centre ring, 4 ds, join to fourth picot of centre ring, 8 ds, join shuttle thread to Ring B, 6 ds, join shuttle thread to Ring A, rw.

Ring A, Chain B and Ring A as before.

Chain E of 9 ds, miss next picot on last Chain C of motif and join to following picot, 6 ds, miss next picot on next motif and join to following picot, 9 ds, join shuttle thread to Ring A, rw.

Repeat from * all along, joining the final chain of the row to match the first. Tie to ring A to finish.

Second Row

Ring of 5 ds, join to first Ring A of First Row, 5 ds, p, 9 ds, rw.
* Chain of 6 ds, p, 6 ds, join shuttle thread to picot of previous ring, rw.

Ring of 5 ds, join to next Ring A of First Row, 5 ds, p, 9 ds, rw.

Repeat from * all along, finishing with a chain tied to the last ring. Thread ribbon as shown.

Annette

Using crochet cotton No. 40, each sprig measures 2 inches (5 cm) in length, and 26 sprigs are appliquéd on cotton net for a collar $3\frac{1}{2}$ inches (9 cm) in width and 17 inches (43 cm) in length. The design can be adapted for a collar of any size or curvature by adjusting the number of sprigs used.

Sprig

Ring A of 7 ds, p, 5 ds, p, 2 ds.
Ring B of 2 ds, join to last picot of Ring A, 7 ds, p, 7 ds, rw.
Chain A of 3 ds, p, 5 ds, p, 7 ds, rw.
Ring C of 3 ds, p, 2 ds, p, 2 ds, join to Ring B, (2 ds, p) 4 times, 7 ds.
Ring D of 7 ds, join to last picot of Ring C, (2 ds, p) 7 times, 3 ds, rw.
Chain B of 25 ds, rw.
Ring E of 3 ds, p, (2 ds, p) 3 times, 2 ds, join to third picot (counting in the order worked) of Ring D, (2 ds, p) 3 times, 7 ds.
Ring F of 7 ds, join to last picot of Ring E, (2 ds, p) 5 times, 7 ds.
Ring G of 7 ds, join to last picot of Ring F, (2 ds, p) 5 times, 3 ds.
Chain C of 7 ds, p, (5 ds, p) twice, 2 ds, p, 5 ds, p, 2 ds, p, 5 ds, p, 7 ds.
Tie to base of centre bud to finish.

Work 25 more sprigs similarly, or the number required.

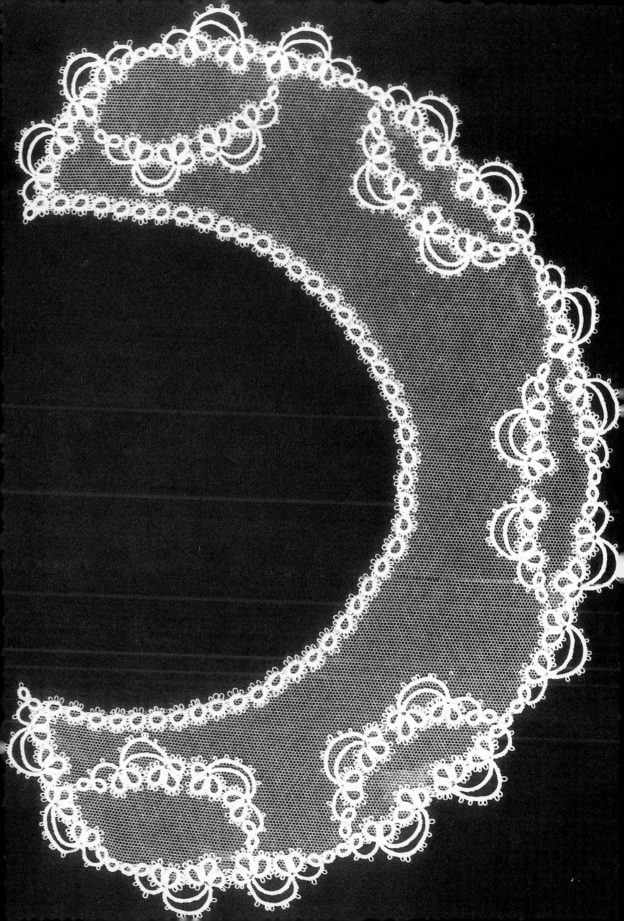

31 Close-up of *Annette*

Edging

Ring of (2 ds, p) 7 times, 1 ds, p, (2 ds, p) twice, 1 ds.

Take shuttle thread to back of ring and join to 7th picot.

Ring of 2 ds, join to 6th picot of previous ring, (2 ds, p) 6 times, 1 ds, p, (2 ds, p) twice, 1 ds.

* Take shuttle thread to back of ring and join to 6th picot.

Ring of 2 ds, join to 5th picot of previous ring, (2 ds, p) 6 times, 1 ds, p, (2 ds, p) twice, 1 ds.

Repeat from * till the edging measures 17 inches (43 cm) or the length required.

To make up

Pre-shrink the net and place a paper pattern under it as a guide for the appliqué. (The net is cut to shape after all the sewing is completed.) Damp the tatting and when dry arrange 16 sprigs in pairs along the outer edge of the collar, with the remaining pairs inside the design as shown. Tack the sprigs into place from the right side of the work, then sew them accurately from the wrong side, leaving all chains loose. Cut away excess net and press lightly from the wrong side.

32 *Carnation*

Carnation

Using crochet cotton No. 20, the flower measures $2\frac{1}{2}$ inches (6.5 cm) in diameter after assembly.

Motif (make two for each flower)
Ring A of 4 ds, p, 6 ds, p, 6 ds, p, 4 ds.
* Ring B of 4 ds, join to last picot of Ring A, 12 ds, p, 4 ds.
Ring C of 4 ds, join to Ring B, 6 ds, p, 6 ds, p. 4 ds, rw.
Chain A of 6 ds, p, 2 ds, p, 2 ds, rw.
Ring D of 6 ds, join to last picot of previous ring, 4 ds, p, 6 ds, rw.
Chain B of (2 ds, p) 5 times, 2 ds, rw.
Repeat Ring D and Chain B once more, then Ring D again.
Chain C of (2 ds, p) twice, 6 ds, rw.
Ring A of 4 ds, join to previous Ring D, 6 ds, join to previous Ring C, 6 ds, p, 4 ds.

Repeat from * four times more.

Ring B as before.
Ring C of 4 ds, join to previous Ring B, 6 ds, join to first Ring A, 6 ds, p, 4 ds, rw.
Chain A, (Ring D, Chain B) twice.
Ring D of 6 ds, join to previous Ring D, 4 ds, join to first Ring A, 6 ds, rw.
Chain C of (2 ds, p) twice, 6 ds.

70

Tie to beginning of motif to finish.

To make up
Wire each motif separately, running fine florist's wire through all Rings B and twisting to form a stem. Place two motifs together and wrap the combined stem with florist's tape.

Cat's Cradle

Using crochet cotton No. 10, the motif measures 3 inches (7.5 cm) across.

First Motif
Ring A of 6 ds, p, (3 ds, p) twice, 6 ds, p, 6 ds.
Chain A of 9 ds, rw.
Ring B of 9 ds, p, 3 ds, p, 6 ds.
Ring C of 6 ds, p, 3 ds, p, 9 ds, rw.
Chain B of 9 ds, join to last picot of Ring A, rw.
Chain C of 11 ds, join to last picot of Ring C, 3 ds, p, 6 ds, p, 3 ds, p, 11 ds, rw.
* Ring A of 6 ds, join to next picot of previous Ring A, (3 ds, p) twice, 6 ds, p, 6 ds.
Chain A as before.
Ring B of 9 ds, join to last picot of Chain C, 3 ds, p, 6 ds.
Ring C, Chain B, Chain C as before.

Repeat from * four times more, joining final Ring A to first Ring A, and joining final Chain C to first Ring B, using the rosette join shown in *Further Techniques*.

Tie to base of first Ring A to finish.

Second Motif
Work Ring A, Chain A, Ring B, Ring C, Chain B as First Motif.
Chain C of 11 ds, join to last picot of Ring C, 3 ds, p, 6 ds, join to corresponding picot of First Motif, 3 ds, p, 11 ds, rw.
Work next Ring A and Chain A as before.
Ring B of 9 ds, join to last picot of Chain C, 3 ds, join to corresponding picot of First Motif, 6 ds.
Ring C of 6 ds, join to corresponding picot of First Motif, 3 ds, p, 9 ds, rw.
Chain B as before.

71

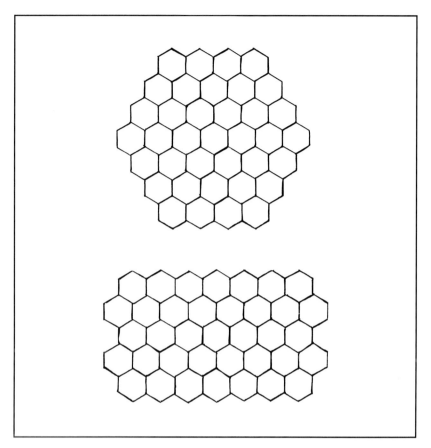

28 A six-sided arrangement of hexagonal motifs

29 A rectangular arrangement of hexagonal motifs

Chain C of 11 ds, join to last picot of Ring C, 3 ds, join to corresponding picot of First Motif, 6 ds, p, 3 ds, p, 11 ds, rw. Complete Second Motif as First Motif.

Motifs are joined on all sides as shown. Hexagonal motifs can be joined concentrically to form a six-sided cloth (Fig. 28), or joined in rows to form a rectangular cloth (Fig. 29).

34 *Cat's Cradle*

Cherry Ripe

Using crochet cotton No. 20, the lace measures $8\frac{1}{2}$ inches (22 cm) in diameter.

First Segment

Ring A of 12 ds, p, 12 ds, rw.
Chain A of 14 ds, p, 6 ds, join shuttle thread to picot of Ring A, 6 ds, p, 14 ds, join shuttle thread to base of same ring, rw.
Chain B of 4 ds, p, 14 ds, rw.
Ring B of 9 ds, p, 3 ds.
Ring C of 3 ds, join to Ring B, 6 ds, p, 6 ds, p, 3 ds.
Ring D of 3 ds, join to last picot of Ring C, 3 ds, p, 6 ds, rw.
Chain C of 10 ds, p, 2 ds, rw.
Ring E of 6 ds, join to Ring D, 6 ds, rw.
Chain D of 2 ds, p, 6 ds, p, 2 ds, p, 8 ds, rw.
Ring F of 6 ds, join to junction of Rings D and E, 3 ds, p, 3 ds.
Ring G of 3 ds, join to previous ring, 12 ds, p, 3 ds.
Ring H of 3 ds, join to previous ring, 3 ds, p, 6 ds, rw.
Chain E of 8 ds, join to last picot of previous chain, 2 ds, p, 8 ds.
Ring A as before.
Chain A of 6 ds, join to Ring H, 8 ds, p, 6 ds, join shuttle thread to Ring A, 14 ds, p, 6 ds, join shuttle thread to base of same ring, rw.
Chain F of 8 ds, join to previous Chain E, 2 ds, p, 8 ds, rw.
Ring F of 6 ds, join to last picot of Chain A, 3 ds, p, 3 ds.
Rings G and H, Chain E and Ring A as before.
Chain A of 6 ds, join to Ring H, 14 ds, join shuttle thread to Ring A, 14 ds, p, 6 ds, join shuttle thread to base of same ring, rw.
Chain F, Rings F, G and H, Chain E and Ring A as before.
Chain A of 6 ds, join to Ring H, 14 ds, join shuttle thread to Ring A, 6 ds, p, 8 ds, p, 6 ds, join shuttle thread to base of same ring, rw.
Chain F, Rings F, G and H as before.
Chain G of 8 ds, join to previous chain, 2 ds, join to corresponding picot of Chain D, 6 ds, join to corresponding picot of Chain D, 2 ds, rw.
Ring I of 6 ds, join to previous Ring H, 6 ds, rw.
Chain H of 2 ds, join to Chain C, 10 ds, rw.
Ring J of 6 ds, join to junction of Rings H and I, 3 ds, p, 3 ds.
Ring K of 3 ds, join to Ring J, 6 ds, p, 6 ds, p, 3 ds.
Ring L of 3 ds, join to Ring K, 9 ds, rw.
Chain I of 14 ds, join to Chain B, 4 ds.

Tie to base of first Ring A to finish.

35 *Cherry Ripe*

Second Segment

Ring A as before.

Chain A of 14 ds, p, 6 ds, join shuttle thread to picot of Ring A, 6 ds, join to corresponding picot of Chain A at beginning of First Segment, 14 ds, join shuttle thread to base of same ring, rw. Chain B and Ring B as before.

Ring C of 3 ds, join to Ring B, 6 ds, join to Ring K of First Segment, 6 ds, p, 3 ds.

Ring D, Chain C, Ring E, Chain D, Rings F, G and H, Chain E and Ring A as before.

Chain A of 6 ds, join to Ring H, 8 ds, join to corresponding picot of Chain A of First Segment, 6 ds, join shuttle thread to Ring A, 14 ds, p, 6 ds, join shuttle thread to base of same ring, rw.

Complete Second Segment as First Segment.

Join a total of 8 segments, connecting the last to the first to complete the design.

Centre Filling
* Ring of 6 ds, join to centre of any Chain A, 6 ds, rw.
Chain of 6 ds, rw.
Repeat from * all around, joining to each Chain A in turn.

Tie to base of first ring to finish.

Chignon Net

Using crochet cotton No. 20, the net measures $5\frac{1}{2}$ inches (14 cm) in diameter but can be enlarged to a full-sized snood if required.

First Round
* Ring of 5 ds, p, 5 ds, p, 10 ds, rw.
Chain of 12 ds, join shuttle thread to last picot of previous ring, rw.

Repeat from * four more times.
Ring of 5 ds, p, 5 ds, join to base of first ring, 10 ds, rw.
Chain of 12 ds, join shuttle thread to same base of first ring.

Second Round
* Chain of 14 ds, join shuttle thread to next junction of chains on previous round.

Repeat from * all around.

Third Round
* Chain of 4 ds, p, (3 ds, p) 3 times, 4 ds, join shuttle thread to next junction of chains.

36 *Chignon Net*

Repeat from * all around, and then abandon the ball thread.

Fourth Round
Join shuttle thread to next picot. Leave a space of $\frac{1}{8}$ inch (3 mm).
Ring of 4 ds, join to same picot, 4 ds. Space of $\frac{1}{2}$ inch (1.25 cm).
* Ring of 4 ds, join to next picot, 4 ds. Space of $\frac{1}{2}$ inch (1.25 cm).

Repeat from * all around, making 24 rings altogether.

Fifth round
* Ring of 4 ds, join to next space of previous round, 4 ds. Space as before.

Repeat from * all around.

Sixth Round
* Ring of 4 ds, join to next space of previous round, 4 ds. Space as before.
Ring of 4 ds, join to same space of previous round, 4 ds. Space as before.
Ring of 4 ds, join to next space of previous round, 4 ds. Space as before.

Repeat from * all around.

Seventh, Eighth and Ninth Rounds
As Fifth Round.

Thread shirring elastic through the final round. To make a larger net, increase as given for the Sixth Round whenever necessary.

Grace and Favour

Using crochet cotton No. 20, each motif measures $1\frac{3}{4}$ inches (4.5 cm) in diameter.

First Motif
Centre rosette:
Ring of 6 ds, p, (2 ds, p) twice, 4 ds, p, (2 ds, p) twice, 6 ds.
* Ring of 6 ds, join to last picot of previous ring, (2 ds, p) twice, 4 ds, p, (2 ds, p) twice, 6 ds.

Repeat from * four times more, joining the last ring to the first (using the method given in *Special Techniques*).

Tie the centre at back of work. Take the two picots on each side of the last junction together as one, and join the shuttle thread to them.

Ring A of 2 ds, p, 3 ds, p, 2 ds.
* Join thread to next picot of rosette.
Ring B of 2 ds, join to last picot of Ring A, 4 ds, p, 6 ds, p, 4 ds, p, 2 ds.
Join thread to next picot of rosette.
Ring A of 2 ds, join to last picot of Ring B, 3 ds, p, 2 ds.
Take the next two picots on each side of the junction together as one, and join thread as before.

Ring A of 2 ds, join to previous Ring A, 3 ds, p, 2 ds.
Repeat from * all around, joining final Ring A to first Ring A.
Tie to junction of picots to finish.

Second Motif
Work as First Motif until first Ring B is reached.
Ring B of 2 ds, join to Ring A, 4 ds, p, 6 ds, join to corresponding
picot of Ring B of First Motif, 4 ds, p, 2 ds.
Work the next two Rings A as before.
Ring B of 2 ds, join to Ring A, 4 ds, join to corresponding picot of
next Ring B of First Motif, 6 ds, p, 4 ds, p, 2 ds.
Complete Second Motif as First Motif.
Further motifs are joined similarly, as shown. See also Figs 28 and
29.

Alternative Motif
Ring A of 8 ds, p, (6 ds, p) 3 times, 8 ds.
* Ring B of 8 ds, join to last picot of Ring A, 4 ds, p, 8 ds.
Ring A of 8 ds, join to Ring B, (6 ds, p) 3 times, 8 ds.
Repeat from * four times more.
Ring B of 8 ds, join to Ring A, 4 ds, join to First Ring A (using the
method given in *Special Techniques*), 8 ds.

Tie at the centre to finish.

This motif joins to the others by the outer picots of Rings A as
shown.

June

Using crochet cotton No. 60, the tatting measures ¾ inch (2 cm) in width and will adapt to a curve. For the streamers, which are an example of Twisted Tatting as shown in Figure 20, use No. 5 or 10 cotton.

Veil Edging
* Ring A of 7 ds, p, 7 ds, rw.
Chain A of 14 ds, rw.
Ring B of 4 ds, p, 2 ds, join to Ring A, (2 ds, p) 4 times, 4 ds.
Ring C of 4 ds, join to last picot of Ring B, (2 ds, p) 4 times, 4 ds, p, 4 ds.
Ring D of 4 ds, join to last picot of Ring C, 4 ds, p, (2 ds, p) 3 times, 4 ds, rw.
Chain B of 30 ds, rw.
Ring E of 9 ds, join to junction of Rings C and D, 5 ds, p, 4 ds.
Ring F of 4 ds, join to Ring E, 5 ds, p, 9 ds, rw.
Chain C of 20 ds, rw.
Ring G of 4 ds, join to Ring F, 7 ds.

Repeat from * for the length required.

To make up the Veil
Cut the net as required and press the tatting under a damp cloth. Tack it to the net from the right side, and stitch neatly (through the junctions of all the rings) from the wrong side, with fine sewing cotton. Press the finished veil lightly.

To make the Net Roses
Cut strips of net 30 inches (76 cm) × 6 inches (15 cm). Fold each in half lengthwise and gather the entire raw edge. Roll each gathered strip into a rose form and stitch securely through the base. Insert fine florist's wire to form a stem and wrap with florist's tape.

Streamers
With the shuttle wound directly from the ball, hang a safety-pin on the thread to provide a hold, and work a half-stitch chain of 20 inches (50 cm) or the length required.

Mittens

Using crochet cotton No. 40, the mittens will fit an average hand, and size is adaptable. To ensure a perfect fit, try each mitten on the hand occasionally while it is being worked, and if necessary adjust the size of the spaces. The elasticated wrists are worked in crochet and both hands are alike.

Make a circle of double shirring elastic to fit around the wrist. Using a fine steel crochet hook, work 110 double-crochet over the elastic. Slipstitch to the first stitch, turn the crochet upside down, and work a second round of 110 double-crochet, inserting the hook between each of the previous stitches. Fasten off but do not cut the thread. Unwind more from the ball and fill the shuttle with the unwound thread. Leave a space of $\frac{1}{8}$ inch (3 mm) before beginning the tatting.

First Round
Ring of 4 ds, join to nearest double-crochet using a normal tatted join, 4 ds. Space of $\frac{3}{8}$ inch (1 cm).
* Ring of 4 ds, miss 4 double crochet of same round, join to next double crochet, 4 ds. Space of $\frac{3}{8}$ inch (1 cm).

Repeat from * all around, making 22 rings altogether.

Second Round
* Ring of 4 ds, join to next space of previous round, 4 ds. Space of $\frac{3}{8}$ inch (1 cm).

Repeat from * all around.

Third Round
As Second Round.

Fourth Round
Ring of 4 ds, join to next space of previous round, 4 ds. Space as before.
Ring of 4 ds, join to same space of previous round, 4 ds. Space as before.
Complete the round in the usual way, as Second Round.

Fifth Round
As Second Round.

Sixth Round
* Ring of 4 ds, join to next space of previous round, 4 ds. Space as before.
Ring of 4 ds, join to same space, 4 ds. Space as before.
Repeat from * once more, then complete the round in the usual way.

Seventh Round
As Second Round.

Eighth Round
Ring of 4 ds, join to next space of previous round, 4 ds. Space as before.
Ring of 4 ds, join to same space, 4 ds. Space as before.
(Ring of 4 ds, join to next space, 4 ds. Space as before) 3 times.
Ring of 4 ds, join to same space, 4 ds. Space as before.
Complete the round in the usual way.

Ninth to Twelfth Rounds
As Second Round.

Thirteenth Round
Miss first 7 spaces of previous round, then complete the round in the usual way.

Fourteenth to Nineteenth Rounds
As Second Round.

After the final ring, reverse work, and take up the ball thread for the edging:
* Chain of 4 ds, p, (1 ds, p) twice, 4 ds, rw.
Ring of 4 ds, join to next space of previous round, 4 ds, rw.

Repeat from * all around, ending with a chain. Tie to start of first chain in order to finish.

The Thumb

First Round
Ring of 4 ds, join to centre ring at back of thumb opening, 4 ds. Space as before.
Ring of 4 ds, join to half space of Twelfth Round, 4 ds. Space as before.
(Ring of 4 ds, join to next space of Twelfth Round, 4 ds. Space as before) 7 times.
Ring of 4 ds, join to half space of Twelfth Round, 4 ds. Space as before.

39 Mittens

Second Round

Ring of 4 ds, join to next space of previous round, 4 ds. Do not leave a space.

Ring of 4 ds, join to next space, 4 ds. Space as before.

Complete the round in the usual way.

Work 3 more rounds in the usual way then work an edging to match the hand.

The Cuff

First Round

Ring A of 6 ds, join to any double-crochet at edge of wrist, 6 ds, rw. Space of $\frac{1}{8}$ inch (3 mm).

Ring B of 5 ds, p, (5 ds, p) twice, 5 ds, rw. Space of $\frac{1}{8}$ inch (3 mm).

* Ring A of 6 ds, miss 3 double crochet, join to next double crochet, 6 ds, rw. Space as before.

Ring B of 5 ds, join to last picot of previous Ring B, (5 ds, p) twice, 5 ds, rw. Space as before.

Repeat from * all around, joining final Ring B to first Ring B, (there should be 27 altogether). Tie to base of first Ring A to finish.

Second Round

Ring C of 6 ds, p, 6 ds, join to any Ring B of First Round, 6 ds, p, 6 ds, rw. Space of $\frac{1}{8}$ inch (3 mm).

Ring D of (5 ds, p) twice, 5 ds, rw. Space of $\frac{1}{8}$ inch (3 mm).

* Ring C of 6 ds, join to last picot of previous Ring C, 6 ds, join to next Ring B of First Round, 6 ds, p, 6 ds, rw. Space as before.

Ring D of 5 ds, join to previous Ring D, 5 ds, p, 5 ds, rw. Space as before.

Ring D of 5 ds, join to previous Ring C, 5 ds, p, 5 ds, rw. Space as before.

Ring E of 6 ds, join to adjacent Ring D, (3 ds, p) 4 times, 6 ds, rw. Space as before.

Ring D of 5 ds, join to adjacent Ring D, 5 ds, p, 5 ds, rw. Space as before.

Ring E of 6 ds, join to last picot of previous Ring E, (3 ds, p) 4 times, 6 ds, rw. Space as before.

Ring C of 6 ds, join to previous Ring D, 6 ds, miss next Ring B of First Round, join to following Ring B, 6 ds, p, 6 ds, rw. Space as before.

Ring D of 5 ds, join to last picot of previous Ring E, 5 ds, p, 5 ds, rw. Space as before.

Repeat from * all around, joining the two final rings to the beginning of the round. Tie to base of first ring to finish.

Third Round

With shuttle wound direct from the ball, tie to first free picot of any pair of Rings E, * Chain of 4 ds, p, (1 ds, p) twice, 4 ds, join shuttle thread to last free picot of same ring.

Chain of 3 ds, join shuttle thread to first free picot of next Ring E.

Chain of 4 ds, p, (1 ds, p) twice, 4 ds, join shuttle thread to last free picot of same ring.

Chain of 6 ds, p, (1 ds, p) twice, 6 ds, join shuttle thread to first free picot of next Ring E.

Repeat from * all around, and tie last chain to first.

Rose Garden

Using crochet cotton No. 20, the motif measures 2¾ inches (7 cm) across.

First Motif

Centre Ring A of (4 ds, p) 5 times, 4 ds. Work lock stitch to form a 6th picot.

Chain A of (6 ds, join shuttle thread to next picot of Ring A) 6 times.

Chain B of (8 ds, join shuttle thread to next picot of Ring A so that join wraps over previous join) 6 times.

Chain C of (10 ds, join as before to next picot of Ring A) 6 times.

Chain D of (4 ds, p, 4 ds, p, 4 ds, join as before to next picot of Ring A) 6 times.

Chain E of 4 ds, join shuttle thread to first picot of Chain D, small picot, 4 ds, join shuttle thread to following picot, 2 ds, rw.

Ring B of 12 ds, (p, 3 ds) 4 times, rw.

Chain F of 6 ds, p, 6 ds, p, 3 ds, join shuttle thread to last picot (counting in the order worked) of Ring B.

* Chain G of 3 ds, join to last picot of preceding chain, (6 ds, p) twice, 3 ds, join shuttle thread to next picot of Ring B.

Chain H as Chain G.

Chain I of 3 ds, join to last picot of Chain H, 6 ds, p, 6 ds, join shuttle thread to remaining picot of Ring B.

Chain J of 2 ds, join shuttle thread to next picot of Chain D, 4 ds, join shuttle thread to following picot, 2 ds, rw.

Ring B as before.
Chain F of 6 ds, join to Chain I, 6 ds, p, 3 ds, join shuttle thread to last picot of Ring B.
Repeat from * four times more.

Chains G and H as before.
Chain I of 3 ds, join to Chain H, 6 ds, join to first Chain F (using the rosette join shown in *Further Techniques*), 6 ds, join shuttle thread to Ring B.
Chain of 2 ds, tie to small picot of Chain E to finish.

Second Motif
Work centre rose, and Ring B, Chain F, Chain G as before.
Chain H of 3 ds, join to last picot of Chain G, 6 ds, join to corresponding picot of First Motif, 6 ds, p, 3 ds, join shuttle thread to next picot of Ring B.
Chains I and J, Ring B and Chain F as before.
Chain G of 3 ds, join to Chain F, 6 ds, join to corresponding picot of First Motif, 6 ds, p, 3 ds, join shuttle thread to next picot of Ring B.
Complete Second Motif as First Motif.

Further motifs are joined similarly as shown. See also Figs 28 and 29.

40 *Rose Garden*

Sicilian Circle

Using crochet cotton No. 10, the lace measures $10\frac{1}{4}$ inches (26 cm) in diameter.

First Round
Ring of 10 ds, p, (5 ds, p) 3 times, 10 ds, rw.
Chain of 3 ds, rw.
* Ring of 10 ds, join to last picot of previous ring, (5 ds, p) 3 times, 10 ds, rw.
Chain of 3 ds, rw.
Repeat from * six times more, joining final ring to first ring (using the method for connecting a rosette). Tie to base of first ring to finish.

Second Round
Ring A of 7 ds, join to any free picot of First Round, 7 ds, rw.
Chain A of 10 ds, mark the position of the last ds by hanging a small safety-pin on the shuttle thread, then continue with 7 ds, p, 3 ds.
Ring B of 3 ds, join to picot of Chain A, 7 ds, p, 5 ds, p, 5 ds.
* Ring C of 5 ds, join to last picot of Ring B, (5 ds, p) twice, 5 ds.
Ring D of 5 ds, join to last picot of Ring C, 5 ds, p, 7 ds, p, 3 ds.
Chain B of 3 ds, join to last picot of Ring D, 7 ds, join shuttle thread to Chain A at position marked, 10 ds, rw.
Ring A of 7 ds, join to next picot of First Round, 7 ds, rw.
Chain A as before.
Ring B of 3 ds, join to Chain A, 7 ds, join to previous Ring D, 5 ds, p, 5 ds.
Repeat from * all around, joining last Ring D to first Ring B (using the method for connecting a rosette), and ending with a final Chain B.
Tie to base of first Ring A to finish.

Third Round
Ring A of 14 ds, p, 2 ds, p, 14 ds, rw.
Chain A of 19 ds, small p, 1 ds, rw, 12 ds, p, 3 ds.
Ring B of 3 ds, join to last picot of Chain A, 10 ds, join to adjacent picot of Ring A, 2 ds, p, 12 ds, p, 3 ds.
Ring C of 3 ds, join to Ring B, 12 ds, join to any Ring C of Second Round, 12 ds, p, 3 ds.
* Ring D of 3 ds, join to Ring C, 12 ds, p, 2 ds, p, 10 ds, p, 3 ds.
Chain B of 3 ds, join to last picot of Ring D, 12 ds, rw, join to small picot of Chain A, 20 ds, rw.
Ring A of 14 ds, join to adjacent picot of Ring D, 2 ds, p, 14 ds, rw.
Chain A as before.

Ring B of 3 ds, join to last picot of Chain A, 10 ds, join to previous Ring A, 2 ds, join to previous Ring D, 12 ds, p, 3 ds.

Ring C of 3 ds, join to Ring B, 12 ds, join to next Ring C of Second Round, 12 ds, p, 3 ds.

Repeat from * all around, joining final Ring D to first Rings B and A, and ending with a final Chain B. Tie to base of first Ring A to finish.

Fourth Round

With shuttle wound directly from the ball, join to base of any Ring A of Third Round.

Chain A of 3 ds, p, 16 ds, p, 3 ds, join shuttle thread to small picot at junction of Chains A and B of Third Round.

Chain B of 3 ds, join to last picot of chain A, 12 ds, p, 12 ds, p, 3 ds, join shuttle thread to same small picot as before (thus making a false ring).

91

Chain A of 3 ds, join to last picot of Chain B, 16 ds, p, 3 ds, join shuttle thread to base of next Ring A.

Chain B of 3 ds, join to Chain A, 12 ds, p, 12 ds, p, 3 ds, join shuttle thread to same base of Ring A as before (making another false ring). Repeat chains A and B in this way all around the circumference, joining final Chain B to first Chain A. Tie to base of first Ring A to finish.

Victoria

Using crochet cotton No. 20, the collar measures $3\frac{1}{4}$ inches (8 cm) in width; length and curvature are adjustable and ribbon can be threaded at the neck edge.

Outer Row

Ring A of (3 ds, p) 4 times, 3 ds, rw.

* Chain A of (6 ds, p) twice, 6 ds, rw.

Ring B of 3 ds, p, 3 ds, join to second picot from the end of Ring A, (3 ds, p) twice, 3 ds, rw.

Chain B of 6 ds, p, 6 ds, rw.

Ring C as Ring A.

Chain C of 3 ds, rw.

Ring D of (3 ds, p) 6 times, 3 ds, rw.

Chain D of 3 ds, rw.

Ring E as Ring A.

Chain E of 6 ds, join to Chain B, 6 ds, rw.

Ring F as Ring A.

Chain F of 6 ds, join to nearest picot of Chain A, 6 ds, p, 6 ds, rw.

Ring A of 3 ds, p, 3 ds, join to second picot from the end of Ring F, (3 ds, p) twice, 3 ds, rw. **

Chain A, Ring B, Chain B, Ring C as before.

Repeat Chain B and Ring C once more.

Chain D, Ring D, Chain D, Ring E, Chain E, Ring F as before.

Repeat Chain E and Ring F once more.

Chain F as before.

Ring A of 3 ds, p, 3 ds, join to Ring F, (3 ds, p) twice, 3 ds, rw. ***

Repeat from * to *** seven times more, or for the length required, then repeat from * to ** once. Do not finish but turn with a chain of 6 ds, rw.

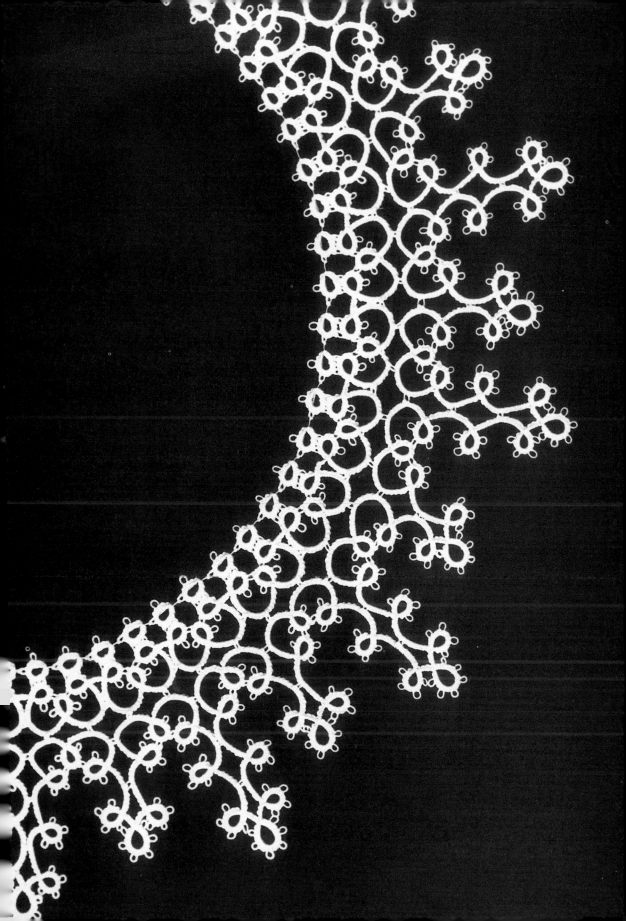

Inner Row

Ring A of (3 ds, p) 4 times, 3 ds, rw.
* Chain A of 6 ds, join to Chain F of Outer Row, 6 ds, p, 6 ds, rw.
Ring B of 3 ds, p, 3 ds, join to second picot from the end of Ring A, (3 ds, p) twice, 3 ds, rw.
Chain B of 3 ds, rw.
Ring C as Ring A.
Chain C of 6 ds, join to Chain A, 6 ds, join to next chain of Outer Row, 6 ds, rw.
Ring A of 3 ds, p, 3 ds, join to second picot from the end of Ring C, (3 ds, p) twice, 3 ds, rw.
Repeat from * all along the row, ending with a turning chain of 6 ds.
Tie to base of first ring of Outer Row to finish.

Edging

Ring of 3 ds, join to first picot on edge of Inner Row, 3 ds, join to next picot of same ring, (3 ds, p) twice, 3 ds.
Take shuttle thread at back of ring just made and join to second picot from the end.
* Ring of 3 ds, join to next picot of following ring on edge, 3 ds, join to next picot of same ring, (3 ds, p) twice, 3 ds.
Take shuttle thread at back of work and join as before.
Repeat from * all along the row.

White Rose†

Using crochet cotton No. 40, the tatting measures approximately $4\frac{1}{2}$ inches (11.5 cm) across each repeat of the pattern, and is designed for a circular veil 48 inches (122 cm) in diameter.

Veil Edging

* Ring A of 12 ds, p, 4 ds.
Ring B of 4 ds, join to Ring A, 12 ds, p, 4 ds.
Ring C of 4 ds, join to Ring B, 12 ds, rw.
Chain A of (4 ds, p) 7 times, 4 ds, rw.
Ring D of 16 ds, rw.
Work (Chain A, Ring D) 3 times more, then Chain A once more.
Repeat from * till the pattern has been worked 32 times altogether.
Tie to beginning, being careful to avoid twisting the work.

43 White Rose

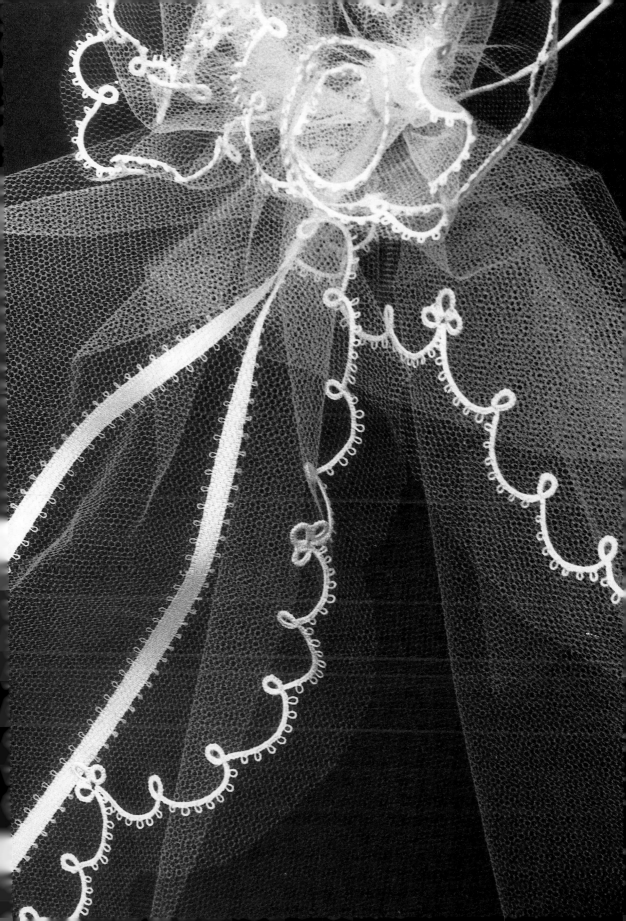

To make up the Veil

Cut a circle of bridal net 48 inches (122 cm) in diameter. Fold it in half three times, thus forming a segment of eight layers. Mark four scallops around the edge of this segment and cut carefully through all the layers. Shrink and press the tatting and attach it, leaving a small margin as shown. Use very fine sewing cotton and sew the base of each ring into place from the back of the work, so that each ring is attached individually, and the chains left free. Press the finished veil lightly.

Rose Edging

Work (Ring D, Chain A) 27 times, and Ring D once more.

To make up the Rose

Cut a strip of net 3 inches (7.5 cm) wide, approximately 28 inches (70 cm) long, and attach the prepared tatting, as given for the veil, along one edge. Gather the opposite edge of the net, roll it into a rose shape, and stitch firmly at the back. Insert fine florist's wire to form a stem and wrap with florist's tape.

Make two roses, or the number required, and mount on a comb.

Windmills

Using crochet cotton No. 20, the motif measures $2\frac{1}{4}$ inches (6 cm) across. This lace is an interpretation in tatting of a favourite nineteenth-century crochet design.

First Motif

With shuttle wound directly from the ball, centre ring of (4 ds, small p) 5 times, 4 ds. Work lock stitch to form a false 6th picot. Centre chain of (2 ds, small p, 2 ds, join shuttle thread to next picot of centre ring, small p) 5 times, 2 ds, small p, 2 ds, join shuttle thread to lock-stitch picot.

First arm:
Chain A of (4 ds, small p) 4 times, 4 ds, rw.
* Chain B of 1 ds, small p, (4 ds, join shuttle thread to next picot of Chain A, small p) 4 times, 5 ds, join shuttle thread to next picot of centre chain, rw.

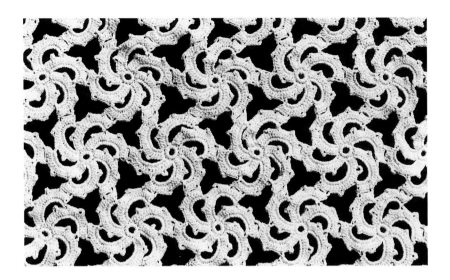

Chain C of (5 ds, join shuttle thread to next picot of Chain B, small
p) 4 times, 5 ds, join shuttle thread to next picot of Chain B, rw.
Chain D of 1 ds, small p, 5 ds, join shuttle thread to next picot of
Chain C, (3 ds, p, 3 ds, join shuttle thread to next picot of Chain C)
3 times, 3 ds, p, 5 ds, join shuttle thread to next picot of centre
chain, rw.

Second arm:
Chain A of (4 ds, small p) 4 times, 4 ds, join shuttle thread to second
picot from centre of previous Chain D, rw.
Repeat from * four more times.
Chains B and C as before.
Chain D of 1 ds, small p, 5 ds, join shuttle thread to next picot of
Chain C, (3 ds, p, 3 ds, join shuttle thread to next picot of Chain C)
twice, 3 ds, join to edge of Chain A of first arm (using the method
for connecting a rosette – shown in *Further Techniques* – only in this
case there is no convenient picot and the hook is inserted through
the chain), 3 ds, join shuttle thread to next picot of Chain C, 3 ds, p,
5 ds.

Tie to lock-stitch picot to finish motif.

Second Motif
Work as First Motif until Chain D of second arm is reached.
Chain D of 1 ds, join to second picot of any Chain D of First Motif,

5 ds, join shuttle thread to next picot of Chain C, 3 ds, join to small picot of same Chain D of First Motif, 3 ds, join shuttle thread to next picot of Chain C, and complete the motif as before.

Further motifs are connected similarly at each arm. See also Figs 28 and 29.

46 Angelica

Angelica

Using crochet cotton No. 40, the lace measures $2\frac{1}{4}$ inches (6 cm) in diameter.

Ring A of 5 ds, p, 2 ds, p, 5 ds.
Ring B of 5 ds, join to last picot of Ring A, (2 ds, p) 3 times, 7 ds, rw.
Ring C of 5 ds, p, 2 ds, p, 5 ds.
* Ring D of 5 ds, join to last picot of Ring C, (2 ds, p) 3 times, 7 ds.
Ring E of 7 ds, join to last picot of Ring D, (2 ds, p) 5 times, 7 ds.
Ring F of 7 ds, join to last picot of Ring E, (2 ds, p) 3 times, 5 ds.
Ring G of 5 ds, join to last picot of Ring F, 2 ds, p, 5 ds, rw.
Ring A of 5 ds, join to last picot of Ring B, 2 ds, p, 5 ds.
Ring B as before.
Ring C of 5 ds, join to Ring G, 2 ds, p, 5 ds.
Repeat from * three times more.

Rings D, E, F, G and A as before.
Ring B of 5 ds, join to previous Ring A, (2 ds, p) twice, 2 ds, join to first Ring A at beginning of round, 7 ds, rw.
Rings C, D, E and F as before.
Ring G of 5 ds, join to Ring F, 2 ds, join to first Ring C (using the method for connecting a rosette), 5 ds.

Tie ends to finish.

Birdcage

Using crochet cotton No. 20, the square measures $2\frac{1}{2}$ inches (6.5 cm) across. Wind the ball thread on a second shuttle to begin the First Round.

Centre
Ring A of 7 ds, p, 7 ds.
Rings B, C and D as Ring A.
Tie at centre to connect the group, and leave a space of $\frac{1}{2}$ inch (1.25 cm) of thread before starting the next group.
* Ring A of 7 ds, join to previous Ring A, 7 ds.
Ring B of 7 ds, join to previous Ring D, 7 ds.
Rings C and D as before.
Join to preceding space to connect the group, then leave a space as before.
Repeat from * twice more, joining final Ring D to first Ring B (using the method for connecting a rosette).
Tie to centre of first group to finish.

First Round
Join to any corner picot.
* Chain of 10 ds, join main shuttle thread to next junction of rings.
Chain of 10 ds, join main shuttle thread to next corner picot.
Repeat from * all around.

Second Round

* Chain of 12 ds, join main shuttle thread to next junction of chains.
Repeat from * all around.

Third Round

* Chain of 14 ds, join as before to next junction of chains.
Using second shuttle: Ring A of 5 ds, p, 5 ds.
Using main shuttle: Chain of 14 ds, join to next junction of chains.
Using second shuttle: Ring B of 7 ds, p, 7 ds.
Rings C and D as Ring B.
Repeat from * all around, changing shuttles as necessary. Tie ends
to finish.

Fourth Round

Join to any Ring A of Third Round.
* Chain of 12 ds, join main shuttle thread to next Ring B.
Chain of 8 ds, join to Ring C.
Chain of 8 ds, join to Ring D.
Chain of 12 ds, join to next Ring A.
Repeat from * all around.

Fifth Round

* Chain of 12 ds, join main shuttle thread to next junction of chains.
Using second shuttle: Josephine Knot of 10 hs.
Using main shuttle: Chain of 8 ds, join to next junction.
Using second shuttle: Josephine Knot as before.
Using main shuttle: Chain of 8 ds, join to next junction.
Using second shuttle: Josephine Knot as before.
Using main shuttle: Chain of 12 ds, join to next junction.
Using second shuttle: Josephine Knot as before.
Repeat from * all around. Tie ends to finish.

Blossom

Using crochet cotton No. 60, the lace measures $1\frac{3}{4}$ inches (4.5 cm) in length; using crochet cotton No. 20, it measures $2\frac{1}{2}$ inches (6.5 cm).

Ring A of 5 ds, p, (2 ds, p) 4 times, 7 ds.
Ring B of 7 ds, join to last picot of previous ring, (2 ds, p) 5 times, 7 ds.
Ring C as Ring B.
Ring D of 7 ds, join to last picot of previous ring, (2 ds, p) 3 times, 7 ds, rw.
Chain A of (5 ds, p) 3 times, 2 ds, join shuttle thread to last picot of Ring D.
Chain B of 2 ds, join to last picot of Chain A, 8 ds, p, 2 ds, p, 5 ds, p, (2 ds, p) twice, (5 ds, p) twice, 5 ds, rw.
Ring E of 3 ds, p, (2 ds, p) 5 times, 7 ds.

Ring F of 7 ds, join to last picot of previous ring, 2 ds, p, 2 ds, join to corresponding picot of Ring C, (2 ds, p) 3 times, 7 ds.
Ring G as Ring B.
Ring H as Ring D.
Chain C of 5 ds, join to last picot of Chain B, (5 ds, p) twice, 5 ds, rw.
Ring I of 7 ds, join to last picot of Ring H, 5 ds, p, 2 ds.
Ring J of 2 ds, join to Ring I, 5 ds, p, 7 ds.

Tie ends to finish.

Bryony

Using crochet cotton No. 60, the lace measures $1\frac{1}{2}$ inches (4 cm) in length; using crochet cotton No. 20, it measures $2\frac{1}{4}$ inches (5.5 cm).

Ring A of 7 ds, p, 7 ds.
Rings B and C as Ring A, rw.
Chain A of (9 ds, p) twice, (2 ds, p) twice, 7 ds, p, 2 ds, (p, 9 ds) twice, rw.
Ring D of 4 ds, p, (2 ds, p) 4 times, 7 ds.
Ring E of 7 ds, join to last picot of previous ring, (2 ds, p) 4 times, 7 ds.
Ring F of 7 ds, join to last picot of previous ring, (2 ds, p) 4 times, 4 ds, rw.
Chain B of 28 ds, p, 9 ds, rw.
Ring G of 4 ds, p, (2 ds, p) 5 times, 7 ds.
Ring H of 7 ds, join to last picot of previous ring, 2 ds, p, 2 ds, join to nearest free picot of Ring E, (2 ds, p) 3 times, 7 ds.
Ring I of 7 ds, join to last picot of previous ring, 2 ds, p, 2 ds, join to Ring B, (2 ds, p) twice, 7 ds.
Ring J of 7 ds, join to last picot of previous ring, (2 ds, p) 5 times, 7 ds.
Ring K of 7 ds, join to last picot of previous ring, (2 ds, p) 5 times, 4 ds.

Tie ends to finish.

Buttercup†

Using crochet cotton No. 60, the lace measures $1\frac{1}{4}$ inches (3.5 cm) in length; using crochet cotton No. 20, it measures $1\frac{3}{4}$ inches (4.5 cm).

Ring A of 7 ds, p, 4 ds, p, 4 ds, p, 7 ds.
* Ring B of 7 ds, join to last picot of previous ring, 4 ds, p, 4 ds, p, 7 ds.
Repeat from * 3 times more, rw.
Chain A of 14 ds, p, 7 ds.
Ring C of 11 ds, p, 7 ds, rw.
Chain B of 5 ds, join to picot at top of last Ring B, 9 ds, rw.
Ring D of 7 ds, join to Ring C, 11 ds.

Tie ends to finish.

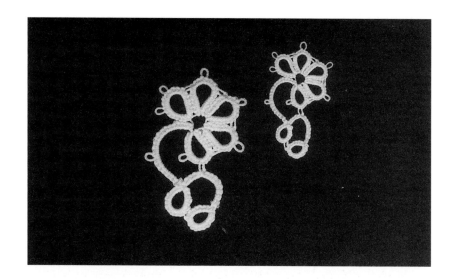

50 *Buttercup*

51 *Corner Spray*

Corner Spray

Using crochet cotton No. 40, the lace measures $2\frac{3}{4}$ inches (7 cm) on its longest edge.

Rosette
Ring A of 7 ds, p, (5 ds, p) twice, 7 ds.
Ring B of 7 ds, join to last picot of previous ring, (5 ds, p) twice, 7 ds.
Ring C as Ring B.
Ring D as Ring B.
Ring E of 7 ds, join to last picot of previous ring, (5 ds, p) twice, 5 ds.

106

Ring F of 5 ds, join to last picot of previous ring. (5 ds, p) twice, 5 ds.
Ring G of 5 ds, join to last picot of previous ring, 5 ds, p, 5 ds, join to first picot of Ring A (using the method given in *Special Techniques*), 7 ds.

Tie ends to finish.

First Leaf Spray
Ring A of (5 ds, p) 3 times, 5 ds.
Ring B of 7 ds, p, 7 ds.
Ring C of 5 ds, p, 5 ds, join to centre picot of Ring F of Rosette, 5 ds, p, 5 ds, rw.
Chain A of 5 ds, join to first picot of leaf Ring A, (5 ds, p) twice, 5 ds, join shuttle thread to junction of Rings D and E of Rosette, rw.
Chain B of (5 ds, p) 3 times, 5 ds, rw.
Ring D of 5 ds, p, 5 ds, join to first picot of Chain A (counting in the order worked), 5 ds, p, 5 ds.
Ring E of 5 ds, join to last picot of previous ring, 5 ds, join to centre picot of leaf Ring A, 5 ds, p, 5 ds.
Ring F of 5 ds, p, (7 ds, p) twice, 5 ds.
Ring G of 5 ds, join to last picot of previous ring, 5 ds.

Tie ends to finish.

Second Leaf Spray
Ring A as First Leaf Spray.
Ring B of 7 ds, join to Ring B of First Leaf Spray, 7 ds.
Ring C of 5 ds, join to corresponding picot of Ring C of First Leaf Spray, 5 ds, join to junction of same ring with Ring F of Rosette, 5 ds, p, 5 ds, rw.
Chain A of 5 ds, join to first picot of leaf Ring A, (5 ds, p) twice, 5 ds, join shuttle thread to junction of Rings G and A of Rosette, rw.

Complete to match First Leaf Spray.

Mayflower

Using crochet cotton No. 60, the lace measures $1\frac{1}{4}$ inches (3.5 cm) in length; using crochet cotton No. 20, it measures $1\frac{3}{4}$ inches (4.5 cm).

Ring A of 7 ds, p, (2 ds, p) 4 times, 7 ds.
Ring B of 7 ds, join to last picot of previous ring, (2 ds, p) 5 times, 7 ds.
Ring C of 7 ds, join to last picot of previous ring, (2 ds, p) 3 times, 7 ds, rw.
Chain A of (5 ds, p) 3 times, 2 ds, join shuttle thread to last picot of Ring C.
Chain B of 2 ds, join to last picot of Chain A, 8 ds, p, 2 ds, p, 5 ds, p, (2 ds, p) twice, (5 ds, p) twice, 5 ds, rw.
Ring D of 3 ds, p, (2 ds, p) 5 times, 7 ds.
Ring E of 7 ds, join to last picot of Ring D, 2 ds, p, 2 ds, join to corresponding picot of Ring B, (2 ds, p) 3 times, 7 ds.
Rings F and G as Ring B.
Ring H as Ring C.

Tie ends to finish.

Rockingham

Using crochet cotton No. 20, the cross measures $4\frac{1}{4}$ inches (11 cm) in height.

Ring A of 8 ds, p, (2 ds, p) twice, 8 ds, rw.
* Chain A of 8 ds, rw.
Ring A of 8 ds, join to last picot of previous Ring A, (2 ds, p) twice, 8 ds.
Ring B of 7 ds, p, 7 ds, rw.
Chain B of 18 ds, p, 2 ds, rw.
Ring C of 7 ds, join to Ring B, 7 ds, rw.
Ring D of 2 ds, join to Chain B, 8 ds, p, 8 ds, p, 2 ds.
Chain C of 2 ds, join to last picot of Ring D, 18 ds, rw.
Ring E of 7 ds, join to junction of Rings B and C, 7 ds.
Ring A of 8 ds, join to last picot of previous Ring A, (2 ds, p) twice, 8 ds, rw.
Repeat from * twice more.

Chain A as before.
Ring A of 8 ds, join to previous Ring A, 2 ds, p, 2 ds, join to first
Ring A, 8 ds.
Ring B, Chain B and Ring C as before (omit Ring D).
Chain C of 2 ds, p, 18 ds, rw.
Ring E as before.
Tie to base of first ring A to finish.

For the stem:
Ring F of 10 ds, join to final Chain C, 2 ds, p, 8 ds.
Ring B, Chain B, Rings C and D, Chain C and Ring E as before.
Ring G of 8 ds, join to Ring F, 2 ds, join to Chain B of main cross,
10 ds.

Tie ends to finish.

Wrought Iron

Using crochet cotton No. 20, the cross measures 5 inches (13 cm) in
height. Wind the ball thread on a second shuttle.

Using main shuttle, start at the base:
Ring A of 10 ds, p, 10 ds, rw.
Chain A of 16 ds, join main shuttle thread to picot of Ring A, small
picot, 16 ds, join main shuttle thread to base of Ring A, turn work
from left to right.
Chain B of 6 ds, p, 16 ds, join main shuttle thread to small picot.

Using second shuttle:
Ring B of 6 ds, p, 6 ds.

Using main shuttle:
Chain C of 16 ds, p, 6 ds, join main shuttle thread to base of Ring A,
rw.
Chain D of 10 ds, p, 12 ds, rw.
Ring C of 6 ds, p, 3 ds, p, 3 ds.
Ring D of 3 ds, join to last picot of previous ring, 6 ds, p, 6 ds, p,
3 ds.
Ring E of 3 ds, join to last picot of previous ring, 3 ds, p, 6 ds, rw.
Chain E of 8 ds, p, 6 ds, rw.
Ring F of 6 ds, p, 6 ds, rw.
Chain F of 10 ds, p, 2 ds, p, 10 ds, rw.

Ring G of 6 ds, join to previous ring, 3 ds, p, 3 ds.
* Rings D and E as before.
Chain F of 10 ds, join to last picot of previous chain F, 2 ds, p, 10 ds, rw.
Ring A, Chain A, as before.
Chain B of 6 ds, join to Ring E, 16 ds, join main shuttle thread to small picot.
Ring B, Chain C as before.
Chain F as previous Chain F.
Ring H of 6 ds, join to Chain C, 3 ds, p, 3 ds.
Repeat from * twice more.

Rings D and E as before.
Chain F of 10 ds, join to previous Chain F, 2 ds, join to first Chain F, 10 ds, rw.
Ring I of 6 ds, join to Ring E, 6 ds, rw.
Chain G of 6 ds, join to Chain E, 8 ds, rw.
Rings C, D and E as before.
Chain J of 12 ds, join to Chain D, 10 ds.

Tie to base of cross to finish.

CHAPTER SIX
Mounting edgings on fabric

There was once a rule among self-respecting needlewomen that hand and machine work should not be mixed. With today's freedom, the two are now not necessarily considered to be incompatible, yet it is a pity, having spent effort on creating the tatting, not to spend a little more on complete hand finishing.

It is safer if both fabric and tatting are shrunk beforehand, as each may shrink at different rates. Steam pressing is usually the most suitable way to shrink and prepare cotton or linen fabrics; the tatting can be damped, or washed as recommended in Chapter 3.

There are many ways of hemming by hand, but whatever method is chosen, the hem should be as narrow as possible, for too wide a hem can overpower a tatted edging. The two following methods are excellent, but need to be well practised first. Crochet cotton is hard and unsympathetic for sewing and a soft embroidery cotton, finer than the cotton used for the tatting, is better.

PUNCH-STITCH HEM

This is a two-stage process, the first row being worked on a single thickness of fabric, the second on a double thickness. The tatting is attached on the second row. Both rows are worked from the front. Use a very large needle for the embroidery, as this will help to punch the threads apart. On an evenweave fabric, count, for example, four threads horizontally and four threads vertically.

To work the first row (Fig. 30):
Working from right to left, and with the raw edge of the fabric at the top, insert the needle from front to back at A, and bring it out at B. Re-insert it at A. It is important that it is re-inserted in precisely the same place as before. Bring the needle out at C and pull the thread slightly. Re-insert the needle at B (again it is essential to use the

55 Punch-stitch hem

same hole) and bring it out at D, re-insert at B and bring it out at E, pulling as before. Continue in this way. The line D–B–A represents the edge of the finished hem.

To work the second row (Fig. 31):
Fold the fabric back at D–B–A, and work through the double layer, from right to left. Insert the needle from the front at F and bring it out at G. Re-insert it at F and take it at the back to B, which is now on the fold. Bring the thread forwards to wrap it over the fold, being careful to align the thread so that it runs diagonally from F to B, and vertically from B to G. Pull slightly. Insert the needle from the front at G and bring it out at H. Re-insert at G and take the thread to D as before. Continue in this way, picking up picots from the tatting as required. Cut away excess fabric at the back afterwards.

DOUBLE-CROCHET HEM

This is also a two-stage process, and in this case, crochet cotton may be use for the hem. The crochet is worked first, then the tatting is sewn to the edge of the crochet afterwards. Alternatively, the tatting can be joined directly to the crochet while the former is being worked, joining in the same way as a normal tatted join.

The hem is worked at the back, on the wrong side. Begin by rolling a narrow double hem and pull a thread from the fabric at the base of this hem. Work double-crochet over the rolled hem, inserting the hook where the thread was removed. If the fabric is an evenweave, count the same number of threads between each

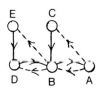

30 First row of punch-stitch

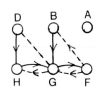

31 Second row of punch-stitch

113

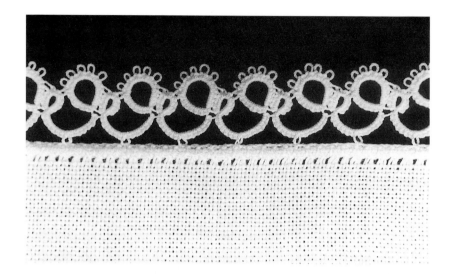

56 Double-crochet hem

57 Curved hem in punch-
stitch

double-crochet. On completion, overcast the heads of each stitch of
the crochet with normal sewing cotton, picking up picots from the
tatting as required.

TO ATTACH TATTING TO A CURVED EDGE

Both methods will adapt to a curve. For a punch-stitch hem, first
mark a curve on the fabric with pencil, to represent the line D–B–A,
then proceed as given before. For a double-crochet hem, work on
the front of the fabric instead of the back (omitting the pulled

thread), and again, mark a curve with pencil. Run a tacking thread along the mark as a stay, as otherwise the edge will tend to stretch. Fold back the fabric once only along the tacking line and work double-crochet, inserting the hook through both layers. Cut away excess fabric at the back afterwards.

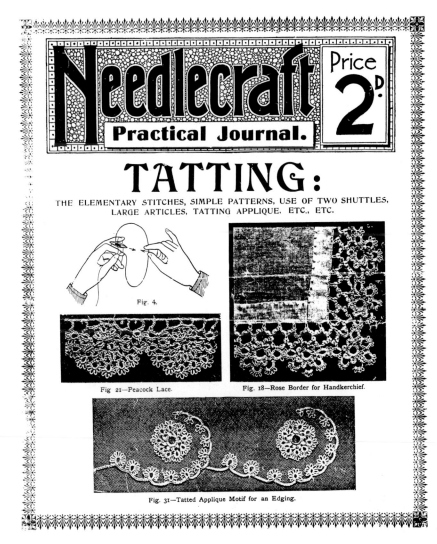

58 A cover from *Needlecraft Practical Journal, 1912*

Bibliography

Bibliography

Further patterns can be found in the following publications:

Anne Orr's Classic Tatting Patterns, Dover Publications, 1985
Attenborough, Bessie M., *The Craft of Tatting*, Bell & Hyman, 1985
Jones, Rebecca, *The Complete Book of Tatting*, Dryad Press/Kangaroo Press, 1985
Konior, Mary, *A Pattern Book of Tatting*, Dryad Press, 1985
Weiss, Rita, *Traditional Tatting Patterns*, Dover Publications, 1986
York, Sheila, *Projects in Tatting*, Dryad Press, 1985

59 A design from *Weldon's Practical Needlework*, 1902

60 A design from Riego's *Complete Tatting Book*, 1865

Historic paintings

depicting ladies with a shuttle

Anne, Countess of Albemarle, by Sir Joshua Reynolds, *circa* 1759, The National Gallery, London
Anne, Countess Temple, by Allan Ramsay, 1760, Chevening, Sevenoaks, Kent
Edward Rookes-Leeds and his family, by Arthur Devis, *circa* 1765, private collection
Francis Vincent and his family, by Arthur Devis, 1763, Harris Museum and Art Gallery, Preston, Lancs
Lepel, Lady Mulgrave, after Johann Zoffany, *circa* 1766, Ickworth House, Bury St. Edmunds, Suffolk
Madame Danger, knotting, by Louis le Tocqué, 1753, The Louvre, Paris
Marie-Adelaide de France, by Jean Marc Nattier, 1756, Versailles
Mrs Seymour Fort, by John S. Copley, *circa* 1776, Wadsworth Atheneum, Hartford, Connecticut
Princess Kunigunde, by Pietro Rotari, 1742, Gemäldegalerie, Dresden
Queen Charlotte and her daughter, by Benjamin West, 1776, Royal Collection, London

32 *Madame Danger*

33 *Princess Kunigunde*

117

34 *Lady Mulgrave*

35 *Mrs Seymour Fort*

61 *Anne, Countess Temple,*
by Allan Ramsay

Suppliers

Shuttles, threads and accessories are available by mail order from:

D. J. Hornsby,
149 High Street,
Burton Latimer,
Kettering,
Northants,
NN15 5RL

Sebalace,
Waterloo Mill,
Howden Road,
Silsden,
West Yorkshire,
BD20 0AH

Galleon Crafts,
72 Church Street,
Whitby,
North Yorkshire

Needlework,
Bucklers Farm,
Coggeshall,
Essex,
CO6 1SB

Lacis,
2982 Adeline Street,
Berkeley,
California 94703,
USA

A. Sells,
49 Pedley Lane,
Clifton,
Shefford,
Bedfordshire

The English Lace School,
Oak House,
Church Stile,
Woodbury,
Devon

Lindalace,
Value House,
12 Union Road,
Croydon,
Surrey,
CRO 2XU

Frivolité,
15526 Densmore N.,
Seattle,
Washington 98133,
USA

Craftsman-made shuttles:

silver from
Rattenburys,
127 Hereson Road,
Ramsgate,
Kent,
CT11 7EE

abalone shell, and other
materials from
Lacis (address above)

Tunbridge Ware from
Peter Benjamin,
11 London Road,
Tonbridge,
Kent,
TN10 3AB

inlaid wood and painted
boxwood from
D. and C. Springett,
21 Hillmorton Road,
Rugby,
Warwickshire,
CV22 5DF

plain polished wood from
A. P. Kingston,
'Erw-Las',
Llanddewi,
Llandrindod Wells,
Powys,
LD1 6SE

flat notched model in polished
wood from
Jack Bamsey,
12 Fir Close,
West Moors,
Wimborne,
Dorset,
BH22 0LF

cotton net from
Needlework (address above)

Index